The Incredible Journey
Mapping the Christian Life

By Dave Martin

DEDICATION

To Terry – for the love, joy and laughter
she's brought to me throughout
our journey as one!

RECOMMENDATIONS
for
THE INCREDIBLE JOURNEY

Reading this book is like sitting in a live audience and hearing great Bible teaching from a dynamic preacher.
Roger Alford, author of *"Pastoring Isn't All It's Cracked Up To be...It's More!"*
President of Walking With God Ministries, Warrenton, Missouri

When we hear the word journey in Christian circles I wonder how many truly understand that the Christian life is indeed an incredible journey?! I wish this book had been written at the beginning of my journey. It may have saved me a ton of pitfalls! What Dave Martin's book does is give us real, relevant and practical advice to enjoy the ride and navigate through the tough times. As a pastor of a church plant, we have a great mix of new and seasoned believers, and I believe this book will be a tremendous resource for both in the years to come! Thank you, Dave, for sharing it with us!
Randy Abbott, Pastor / Founder Misfits for Jesus, St. Louis, Missouri

In The Incredible Journey *author Dave Martin clearly presents the Christian's faith adventure with vivid word pictures. Scripture abounds as the foundation of each life principle. With winsome expression the author connects deep spiritual truth in a fresh, rapid-fire way that invites reflection and personal response.*
Sherry Blankenship, D. Min. Lead Chaplain, Missouri Baptist Medical Center
Author of *Draw Near: One Pilgrim's Journey through Grief to the Lap of Jesus*

In The Incredible Journey *I found answers to questions I didn't even know I was asking. Dave Martin shows you how to engage with a person and then follow up by showing them how to take "The Incredible Journey". The most valuable take-away for me is having the language to pass along to new Christians and those who are seeking the Christ they don't even understand they are trying to find.*
Palmer (Pam) Reynolds, Founder and CEO- Phoenix Textile Corporation, O'Fallon, Missouri

THE INCREDIBLE JOURNEY
Mapping the Christian Life

How's your spiritual journey going? Feel like you're stuck in the mud? Carrying lots of baggage? Maybe gotten off the path, lost your way? Then this book is for you! We've got the Map, and we know the Guide! Come along and discover what it means to be on this incredible journey called the Christian life!

Being a Christ-follower is like a journey that often leads to unexpected places. And, like any adventure, we're often faced with challenges and opportunities at various times in our lives. Somehow the journey seems easier when we travel together, so let's discover together all that we can about *The Incredible Journey!*

Table of Contents

THE INCREDIBLE JOURNEY
Mapping the Christian Life
-Chapter 1-
Knowing God: The Journey Begins

What comes to mind when you think of, or hear the words, "Incredible Journey"? Would it be something like:

The World Equestrian Games of 2010?

Or the Girl Scouts 100th Anniversary in 2012 in Savannah, GA?

Or when St. Louis celebrated the 200th Anniversary of the Lewis & Clark-Expedition Journey back in 2004?

Well, for sure, any and all of these would certainly qualify as incredible journeys. And yet, the Christian life would – or should- qualify as THE Incredible Journey simply because it affects and impacts both this life and the next, both time and eternity.

So what would be the first "step" on this journey?

Well, since it's all about one's spiritual journey, it

has to be' knowing God'. And yet, what does it really mean for someone to "know God"? Because as noted author and theologian J.I. Packer asks, when we talk about *"'knowing God?'.... [Are we talking about an] emotion? A dreamy...floating feeling? [An] intellectual experience? Does one hear a voice, see a vision?"* Because while it is true that our mind, will and emotions are typically involved in knowing anything, there is an eternity's difference between knowing *about* God and *knowing* God.

And then to illustrate his point he goes on to say, *"As it would be cruel to an Amazonian tribesman to fly him to London, put him down without explanation in Trafalgar Square and leave him, as one who knew nothing of English and England, to fend for himself, so we are cruel to ourselves if we try to live in this world without knowing...the God whose world it is and who runs it. The world becomes a strange, mad, painful place and life in it is a disappointing and unpleasant business, for those who do not know...God. Disregard [God] and you sentence yourself to stumble and blunder through life blindfolded with no sense of direction and no understanding of what surrounds you. [If you do this you'll] waste your life and lose your soul."*

Now, perhaps we should ask, though, before we even embark on this journey, "Does God even want to be known? That is, by us?"
Well, consider what God Himself says:

"'You are My witnesses,' says the LORD. 'And My servant whom I have chosen, That you *may know* and believe Me, And understand that I am He. Before Me there was no God formed, Nor shall there be after Me. I, even I, am the LORD, And besides Me there is no savior.'"
[Isaiah 43:10-11, NKJV, emphasis added.]

And then Jeremiah records:

"This is what the Lord says: 'Let not the wise man gloat in his wisdom, or the mighty man in his might, or the rich man in his riches. Let them boast in this alone: that t*hey truly know me* and understand that I am the Lord who is just and righteous, whose love is unfailing and that I delight in these things. I, the Lord, have spoken!'"
[Jeremiah 9:23-24, NLT, emphasis added.]

And then Daniel adds that "...the people that *know their God* shall be strong, and carry out great exploits." [Daniel 11:32b, NKJV, emphasis added.]

And then the Old Testament prophet Hosea adds, "Oh, that we might *know the Lord*! Let us press on to *know him*!" [Hosea 6:3, NLT, emphasis added.]

In a bit I'll expand on what this "knowing" actually involves. For now, though, I think we can see that, from God's perspective, "knowing God" is the first step when it comes to this "Incredible Journey" known as the Christian life.

And yet, as noted earlier, what does "knowing God" actually involve? Well, it has to involve...

FINDING THE GOD WHO IS SEEKING US

Now, the reason for putting the word "finding" in quotes is because [again], as J.I. Packer points out, *"We do not make friends with God; God makes friends with us."* [Emphasis his.]

And this is precisely the point Paul makes. First in Romans he says, "No one is good – not even one. No one is truly wise; no one is seeking God." [Romans 3:10b-11, NLT] And then again in Galatians, "And now that God knows you, why do you want to go back again and become slaves once more to the weak and useless spiritual powers of this world?" [Galatians 4:9, NLT]

Have you ever played "hide and seek"? If we can't find someone, what do we end up saying? *"Come out, come out, wherever you are!"* Well, a lot of people think God is playing some sort of cosmic game of "hide-and-seek"; that it's as if He's crouched behind a bush saying "You're getting warmer, you're getting warmer" as we fumble and stumble around in the dark trying to find Him! He isn't. In fact, God even tells us that "You will seek Me and find Me when you seek Me with all your heart." [Jeremiah 29:13, NIV]

So the real question for us is: are we being wholehearted in our desire to know God, or only half-hearted?

And yet, what sort of God *is* God if and when we do "find" Him – or rather, are "found" by Him? What is He like? Well, He's a great deal more than most people think and realize. He's:

- Immanent [Acts 17:27; the word means "God is near"; thus He's not, as one song puts it, looking at us "from a distance"];

- Omnipresent [Psalm 139:8; God is everywhere];

- Omniscient [Hebrews 4:13; hence God knows everything]; so He's

- Never Surprised [Psalm 139:2-4; He never says "Oh?" Or "Oh, oh!"]; He's

- All-Sufficient [Acts 17:25; thus He has no needs];

- Almighty [Psalm 147:4-5; thus His power is absolute];

- Omnipotent [Jeremiah 32:17; God can do anything];

- Transcendent [1 Kings 8:27; that is, He's greater than His creation];

- Holy [Isaiah 6:1-3; that is, in His purity He is separate from us];

- Compassionate [Lamentations 3:22; He suffers with us];

- Faithful [Hebrews 10:23b; He keeps His word];

- Good [Psalm 106:1; morally, and in every other regard];

- Just [Isaiah 30:18b; He never makes a mistake]; a

- God of wrath [Romans 2:5b-8; fully justified in dealing with sin and sinners], and; a

- God of love [John 3:16; He doesn't just loves us; by nature He is love; cf., 1 John 4:16].

And though Jesus – who is God-in-the-flesh [cf., John 1:1] – reminds us that "People can't come to me unless the Father who sent me draws them to me" [John 6:44a, NLT] we get something of the balance in this divine-human drama.

That is, we see here what God's part is and what our part is when David prays, "When You said, 'Seek my face,' *my* heart said to You, 'Your face, LORD, I will seek.'" [Psalm 27:8, NKJV, emphasis added.] And as Peter reminds us, "He does not want anyone to perish, so he is giving more time for everyone to repent." [2 Peter 3:9b, NLT]

And yet, what does God use to help us "find" – or better, "be found" – by Him? Well, God reveals and makes Himself "findable" in a number of ways:

- Creation / Nature [Psalm 19:1-2],

- History [which is actually "His-story"; Acts 17:26-27],

- Humanity / people [Ecclesiastes 3:11b; we "hear Him" in ours / others' "story"],

- Scripture / The Word of God [2 Peter 1:20-21], and especially the

- Lord Jesus Himself [John 5:39; 14:9].

And, since Solomon tells us that "He has planted eternity in the human heart..." [Ecclesiastes 3:11b, NLT] it's evident that we are "hard-wired" for God; it's part of our spiritual DNA.

It's almost as if we have a "homing device" built within us, causing us to long for home, for heaven. We may try to ignore it or disguise it; we may try to bury it under a myriad of activities, "things", relationships, and even religion. But the Lord of glory will not be ignored; He will intersect our lives countless times along the way, and we'll ultimately meet Him at the end of our journey. [Cf., Hebrew 4:13; 9:27]

And yet, along with our "finding" the God who's seeking us, there's something of a second "step" when it comes "knowing God" and that is:

"KNOWING" THE SAVIOR WHO FOUND US

Now, we read where Jesus tells us that "The Son of Man came to look for [NKJV, "seek"] and to save people who are lost." [Luke 19:10, CEV]And while as children – or adults teaching children – we love to sing, *"Jesus loves me, this I know"*, there's a lot more to our "knowing" this Savior who's found us than may first meet the eye.

This is why quote marks are placed around the word "knowing". Because [again] salvation and / or one's spiritual formation and growth entails a *relationship with* God, not a *religion about* God. Take Paul's words where he says: "Yes, everything else is worthless when compared with the priceless gain of *knowing Christ* Jesus my Lord. I have discarded everything else, counting it all as garbage, so that I may have Christ." [Philippians 3:8, NLT, emphasis added.]

Then, just two verses later he adds, "As a result, I can really *know Christ* and experience the mighty power that raised him from the dead. I can learn what it means to suffer with him, sharing in his death." [Philippians 3:10, NLT, emphasis added.]

And then the Apostle John adds that:

"We know that we have *come to know him* [how?] If we obey his commands. The man who says *'I know him,'* but does not do what he commands is a liar and the truth is not   in him." [1 John 2:3-4, NIV, emphasis added.]

And then later he adds, "But anyone who does not love *does not know God* – for God is love." [1 John 4:8, NLT, emphasis added.]

Can we see what the writers of Scripture are saying? Again, we may *"know a lot* about *Jesus"*, but this isn't the same as our "knowing" Him.

This is why even Jesus asks His followers:

"'Who are the people saying I am?' 'Well,' they replied, 'some say John the Baptist; some Elijah; some, Jeremiah or one of the prophets.' Then He asked them, 'Who do you think I am?' Simon Peter answered, 'The Christ the Messiah, the Son

of the living God.'" [Matthew 16:13-16, LB]
Excellent! And yet, there are a number of
opinions – both then and now – as to who or
what Jesus is. For instance, some still only see or
think of Him in some of the following ways:

- teacher / rabbi [John 3:2],

- "good man" [John 7:12],

- demon possessed [John 7:20],

- sinner [John 9:24],

- "Good Master" [Luke 18:18],

- "do-gooder" [Acts 10:38],

- Prophet [John 4:19; 9:17],

- Son of Joseph [John 1:45],

- Son of David [Mark 10:47],

- Son of Man [Matthew 16:13], and, yes,
  the
- Son of God [John 9:35].

And yet, we can still know – and believe – all

these truths about Jesus [as God] and still not "know" Him. After all, Satan believes all the above! As James tells us, "Do you still think it's enough just to believe that there is one God? Well, even the demons believe this, and they tremble in terror!" [James 2:19, NLT]

So while Satan may be convinced as to who Jesus is, he certainly isn't converted.

And yet, in our case, when it comes to the person of Jesus, almost 9 out of every 10 adults believe that He died and rose again and is alive today. In fact, according to one survey, 3/4ths of all adults state that forgiveness of sins is possible only through Christ! Amazing! And yet, 6 out of 10 do not have any personal assurance of their own eternal destiny or eternal salvation.

So let's do a little word study here.

The Hebrew word for "know" is *"yada"*. One place it's found is Genesis 4:1 where it says, *"Adam knew Eve"*. It means *"to know intimately."* The New Testament word that most closely corresponds to the Old Testament word is the Greek term *"ginosko"*, which means *"to know intimately, personally, not just cerebrally, but by experience"*

So, we're back to the original question: do you "know God"? Or do you just know *about* Him?

And yet, along with our "finding God" and "knowing" Jesus, our "spiritual journey" will then finds us...

DISCOVERING THE REALITY OF ETERNAL LIFE

Now, one might say that there's a sense in which everyone possesses *"immortal* life" – that is, we will live forever, somewhere.

As Paul puts it, "He will give *eternal* life to those who persist in doing what is good, seeking after the glory and honor and *immortality* that God offers." [Romans 2:7, NLT, emphasis added.]

We can have immortal life in heaven or immortal death in hell. However, what Jesus offers us is *"eternal* life" – as opposed to immortal (or eternal) death. So, what or when does "eternal life" begin?

Well, the word itself means perpetual and *"never ending".* And it begins is the very moment we give our heart and life to Christ!

Look at how Jesus puts it: "So that *everyone* who believes in me will have *eternal life.*" [John 3:15, NLT, emphasis added.]

Then later we read where "Simon Peter replied, 'Lord, to whom would we go? You alone have the words that give *eternal life.'*" [John 6:68, NLT, emphasis added.] And as Jesus tells us:

"I give them *eternal life* and they will never perish. No one will snatch them away from me, for my Father has given them to me and he is more powerful than anyone else. So no one can take them from me. The Father and I are one." [John 10:28-30, NLT, emphasis added.]

Then, in what's called His High Priestly prayer, Jesus adds: "For you have given him authority over everyone in all the earth. He gives *eternal life* to each one you have given him. And this is the way to have *eternal life* – to *know* you, the only true God and Jesus Christ, the one you sent to earth" [John 17:2-3, NLT, emphasis added.]

And finally, the Apostle John adds: "So whoever has God's Son has life; whoever does not have his Son, does not have life. I have written this to you who believe in the Son of God so that you may *know* you have *eternal life.*" [1 John 5:12-13,

LB, emphasis added.]

Again, in the Greek language of the New Testament, to *"know"* is an emphatic verb. Thus our salvation isn't a "hope so", "think so", or a "maybe" salvation, but rather a "know so" salvation; a "knowing" that we have eternal life.

Now, again, while surveys report that 85% of Americans consider themselves to be Christians, and over 30% define themselves as "born again", this begs the question as to what it is that makes someone a Christian or "born again"; a possessor of "eternal life" in the first place? Is it our:

- Cultural heritage ("born in 'Christian' America")?
- Our religious tradition or "label"?
- Personal morality?
- Being "good" enough or better than others?
- Keeping the Ten Commandments [or at least the "Top 8"?!]
- Baptism or Confirmation?
- Keeping the Golden Rule?
- Church membership?

No. None of the above. It all has to do with what we do with and about Jesus. And, as John tells us, "But to all who believed him and accepted him,

he gave the right to become children of God."
[John 1:12, NLT]

So, can you remember a time when you first
gave your heart and life to Him? If you haven't
yet, you can now.

And yet, once eternal life is ours, then we'll find
our "journey" underway as we start...

EXPERIENCING A LIFETIME OF
FOLLOWING JESUS

And, as Jesus tell us, "If any of you wants to be
my follower, you must put aside your selfish
ambition, shoulder your cross daily and follow
me.'" [Luke 9:23, NLT] And as Luke records it:

"Peter said, 'We have left our homes and
followed you.' 'Yes,' Jesus replied, 'And I assure
you, everyone who has given up house or wife or
brothers or parents or children, for the sake of
the Kingdom of God, will be repaid many times
over in this life [and Matthew 19:29, NKJV, adds,
"shall receive a hundredfold"] as well as
receiving eternal life in the world to come.'"
[Luke 18:28-30, NLT]
Now, there are many aspects to the Christian life

that can and do help facilitate spiritual growth: worship, Bible studies, ministry, stewardship, serving, etc. However, if that's all we're doing and we're not growing more in love with the Lord Jesus, then we may end up being quite religious, but still lack the vibrancy of a growing, healthy relationship with the Lord.

So, as John tells us:

"What marvelous love the Father has extended to us! Just look at it– we're called children of God! That's who we really are. But that's also why the world doesn't recognize us or take us seriously because it has no idea who he is or what he's up to. But friends, that's exactly who we are: children of God. And that's only the beginning. Who knows how we'll end up! What we know is that when Christ is openly revealed, we'll see him – and in seeing him, become like him." [1 John 3:1-2, MSG]

So why not let this day be the "first day" of the rest of your life; the day when your "Incredible Journey" with Jesus Christ really begins!

It can be, and will be, if you'll let this prayer be your prayer:
"Dear Jesus, thank You for making me and loving

me, even when I've ignored You and gone my own way. I realize I need You in my life and I'm sorry for my sins. I ask You to forgive me. Thank You for dying on the cross for me. Please come into my heart and life and make me a new person inside. Help me to understand what it means to truly belong to You. As much as I know how, I want to follow You for the rest of my life. I accept Your gift of salvation. Please help me to grow now as Your child."

Let the journey begin!

THE INCREDIBLE JOURNEY
Mapping the Christian Life
-Chapter 2-
The Past: What's in Your Backpack?

So, what do people put into their backpacks? Well, we haul all kinds of stuff on our backs and over our shoulders: school supplies, camping gear, and computers, sports equipment, you name it. In fact, another use of backpacks came up a few years back with the movie *Up in the Air* starring George Clooney. In it he plays a motivational speaker who flies around giving talks on the topic, *"What's in Your Backpack?"*

And using backpacks as a metaphor, Clooney's character relates how our "backpacks" are filled with commitments, possessions, family members, friends and *"significant others"* that *"weigh us down"* [because for Clooney's character in the movie, they weigh him down].

Well, we too are going to use "backpacks" as a metaphor or visual aid, only we're going to use them as a container of our past. And perhaps this is something of what Paul has in mind that he *isn't* going to let happen to him. Consider his words when he writes:
"Dear brothers and sisters, I am still not all I

should be, but I am focusing all my energies on this one thing: Forgetting the past and looking forward to what lies ahead, I strain to reach the end of the race and receive the prize for which God, through Christ Jesus, is calling us up to heaven." [Philippians 3:13-14, NLT]

Paul gets it. Do we?

Well, let's consider this second truth or aspect of the Christian life – this Incredible Journey – in light of the previous chapter by first of all...

REVISITING WHAT MAKES US CHRIST-FOLLOWERS

In other words, let's take a backward look at what actually makes us Christians [i.e., believers, "saved" or "born again"], because as Paul puts it, "He saved us in his mercy, not by virtue of any moral achievement of ours, but by the cleansing power of a new birth." [Titus 3:5, Modern English]

What we see is this: that Christianity – this Incredible Journey – is both begun and sustained by God's grace. We can neither add nor subtract anything from it to make it happen. As I like to remind people, "Grace is God *giving to me* that which I *do not* deserve, and mercy is God *not giving to me* that which I *do* deserve." And both are available to everyone.

You see, God really does love us, accept us, and will forgive us regardless of our...

- race or ethnic origin,

- whether rich or poor,

- graduating Magna Cum Laude, or "Lordy, how come?"

- man or woman,

- married or single,

- divorced or widowed,

- young or old,

- a "good" person or the worst sinner around.

As Paul tells us:

"You are living a brand new kind of life that is

continually learning more and more what is right and trying constantly to be more and more like Christ who created this new life within you. In this new life one's nationality or race or education or social position is unimportant; such things mean nothing. Whether a person has Christ is what matters and *he is equally available to all."* [Colossians 3:10-11, LB, emphasis added.]

And yet, while this is how the Incredible Journey – the Christian life – begins, this isn't where it ends. Which is why, when it comes to "backpacks"; we also need to begin...

UNDERSTANDING WHY WE ARE STRUGGLING

You see, over the years I've heard some people say – and some preachers misrepresent – what the gospel really means. [In both cases they're guilty of "overselling the product".] They'll often say something like:

"If you'll just 'give your heart to Jesus' and accept Christ as your Lord and Savior, why, all your sins will be forgiven [very true], *and all your problems will be solved* [not always true]; *you'll be a brand*

new person with a new nature, new heart and new life [all true], *and all your problems will be solved!"* Right. How's that workin' for you?

OK, so why *are* we still struggling? Maybe a story will help. [Whether apocryphal or true it makes the point.]

There was a missionary who approached a Native American and, sharing Christ with him, the man gave his heart and life to Christ. After that, the missionary left for other parts of the country. About a year or so later the missionary returned to check up on the places and people where he'd been, and he came across this Native American.

After asking this relatively new Christian what it's been like being a child of God, the man answered, *"It's like having a black dog and white dog fighting on the inside of me!"* To which the missionary asked, *"Well, which dog wins?!"* And the man answered, *"The one I feed the most!"* Ah yes!

This is why Paul says that "The old sinful nature loves to do evil, which is just opposite from what the Holy Spirit wants. And the Spirit gives us desires that are opposite from what the sinful nature desires. These two forces ["dogs" if you please] are constantly fighting each other and your choices are never free from this conflict." [Galatians 5:17, NLT]

This is also why Paul adds that:

"I do not understand what I do. For what I want to do I do not do, but what I hate I do....What a wretched man I am! Who will rescue me from this body of death? Thanks be to God – through Jesus Christ our Lord!" [Romans 7:15, 24, NIV]

Can anybody relate?! Aren't there times when we actually feel as if we're spiritual schizophrenics; sort of like a Dr. Jekyll and Mr. Hyde? I know I have! Why? Because the Bible [the "Map" or, as is it's often called, "God's Owner's Manual"] says that our struggle is between the "flesh" [or "old man"] and "new man."

Again, here's how Paul describes the "flesh": "The old sinful nature loves to do evil, which is just opposite from what the Holy Spirit wants." [Galatians 5:17a, NLT] Then, a few strokes of the pen later, he adds that: "When you follow your own wrong inclinations, your lives will produce these evil results: impure thoughts, eagerness for lustful pleasure, idolatry, spiritism [that is, encouraging the activity of demons], hatred and fighting, jealousy and anger, constant effort to get the best for yourself, complaints and criticisms, the feeling that everyone else is wrong except those in your own little group. And there will be wrong doctrine, envy, murder, drunkenness, wild parties and all that sort of thing. Let me tell you again as I have before, that anyone living that sort of life will not inherit the Kingdom of God." [Galatians 5:19-21, LB]

On the other hand, Paul identifies the "new man" when he writes that "Those who become Christians become new persons. They are not the same anymore, for the old life is gone. A new life has begun!" [2 Corinthians 5:17, NLT] And then in Galatians he adds, "But when the Holy Spirit controls our lives he will produce this kind of fruit in us: love, joy, peace, patience, kindness, goodness, faithfulness, gentleness and self-control." [Galatians 5:22-23, LB]

OK. So, once we understand, then, what it means to be a Christian or Christ-follower, and why we're still struggling, now we need to begin...

UNPACKING THE "STUFF" WE'RE HIDING

And here I'm talking about what's "below the surface"; what's "out of sight", "off the grid", "under the radar" – our past. Again, it's what's in our "backpack". Because the one thing about our past is that we all have one. And if the truth be known, we do tend to "hide" our "stuff"! As Chuck Swindoll notes Mark Twain as saying *"Everyone is a moon, and has a dark side which he never shows to anybody."*

You see, it isn't too long after we begin this "Journey" that we become painfully aware that some, or many parts, of our past still come back and begin to haunt us. Perhaps we're experiencing flashbacks, or maybe even fantasies, of our past, so we try to suppress, repress, deny or ignore them....which is a little like trying to ignore a flat tire.

Or we opt to "fake it till we make it"; you know, just act as though everything's hunky-dory, couldn't be better! So, when we meet people in the church lobby and they ask, "How ya doin'? And we say, "Great! Wonderful! Hallelujah! I'm just praisin' Jesus!"

Right. [*"Liar, liar, pants on fire!"*]

So, we begin living in fear – fear of disclosure,

discovery; of being "found out." That's why I think churches can learn a lot from therapy groups. I've actually started out a worship service with the words, "Hi, I'm Dave, and I'm a sinner." [Those familiar with therapy groups typically chime back, "Hi, Dave"!]

Well, I want you to hear this: that God does know you and that you're normal! In fact, it's because certain behavior, attitudes, choices, actions, thoughts, and speech actually bother us that should let us know that we really are saved and belong to God.

You see, the closer we are to "The Light", the more clearly we see the "dirt".

Again, as Paul put it earlier, "The sinful nature desires what is contrary to the Spirit and the Spirit what is contrary to the sinful nature. They are in conflict with each other, so that you do not do what you want." [Galatians 5:17, NIV]

And yet, by His grace and power, our dying to self and surrendering each day to the Spirit's control, we will do what He wants us to do! Then, on the "hope-side" of things, Paul writes later that "There is therefore now no condemnation for those who are in Christ Jesus."

[Romans 8:1, RSV]

So, what are we lugging around in our mental, emotional "backpacks"? Let's imagine we're carrying rocks around in them.

That's right, rocks. That's what happens in *The Parent Trap.* In a camping scene the twins Annie and Hallie (played by Lindsay Lohan) are trying to discourage their prospective and hoping-to-marry-money step-mother Meredith Blake (played by Elaine Hendrix). They plot her demise by filling her back-pack with rocks, thus weighing her down to wear her out.

And it works.

So what sort of "rocks" are we carrying around? Well, for some of us, it maybe "rocks" of...

REGRETS

You see, even through *"The Voice"* – Frank Sinatra – may have crooned about his having lived life *"my way"*, and that, regarding "regrets", *"I've had a few..."*, the truth is closer to what John Greenleaf Whittier once wrote:

"For of all sad words

of tongue or pen,
the saddest are these:
'It might have been."

This is when we find ourselves being consumed by the *woulda, coulda, and shoulda's* of life; when all we seemingly think or talk about are the "if-onlys"; the "what might have been"; about:

- vacations not taken,
- kids not valued,
- spouses not appreciated,
- gentleness not expressed,
- retirement not prepared for,
- opportunities not taken,
- gifts not shared,
- sins not forsaken, and
- God not taken seriously enough sooner.

Well, while He certainly wants us to *learn* from our past, God never intends for to *live* in it or be paralyzed *by* it. Again, our response needs to be like that of Paul's where he says, "I can assure you, I am far from thinking that I have already won [that is, that I've "made it" spiritually; that I've "finally arrived"!] All I can say is that I forget the past and I strain ahead for what is still to come."[Philippians 3:13-14, Jerusalem Bible]

Now, to "forget" doesn't mean he develops

amnesia! What it simply means is that that he's not going to "live life staring in the rear view mirror". You see, if you do that long enough you'll end up wrecking your life by "crashing" into what's in front of you.

And yet, along with our regrets, we also carry in our mental and emotional "backpacks" a big old "rock" of...

GUILT

From what? From our regrets, mistakes, sin, any "unfinished business", errors in judgment, what other people have done to – or think about – us, which does have a way of "feeding" or "fueling" this feeling. It was the famous psychiatrist, Dr. Karl Menninger, who once noted that if he could convince his patients that their sins really were forgiven, 75% of them could walk out of the psychiatric hospitals the next day.

And yet, we keep on "replaying the tapes", the CD's and DVD's of "yesterdays failures". We "house" secrets we never share, pain we never reveal, scars we never discuss. And though our faces may reflect joy and delight, inside we're dying a thousand deaths.

We forget – or perhaps we never knew – the truth expressed by Paul in 2 Corinthians 1:3 [KJV], of how God is "the Father of mercies and the God of all comfort."

And how, as Peter tells us, "Casting the whole of your care – all your anxieties, all your worries, all your concerns, once and for all – on Him; for He cares for you affectionately, and cares about you watchfully [Psalm 55:22]." [1 Peter 5:7, Amplified Bible]

This is why all of us need, from time to time, to be reminded of certain "spiritual realties". Like what?" you may ask. Like the one expressed by David where he says, "He has removed our sins as far away from us as the east is from the west." [Psalm 103:12, LB]

Now here the Hebrew word for "removed" is *"nasa"*, which literally means *"up and away"*. Ah, so now when imagining God removing our sins you think of the Space Shuttle taking off from... NASA! *"Up and away!"* And as the Old Testament prophet Isaiah puts it, "You have cast all my sins behind your back." [Isaiah 38:17b, New Revised Standard]
And then there's his fellow prophet Micah who writes, "You will again have compassion on us;

you will...hurl all our iniquities into the depths of the sea." [Micah 7:19, NIV] To which Corrie ten Boom once said that over that spot God posts a sign that reads: *"No Fishing Allowed".*

And yet, along with our regrets and guilt, sometimes our mental and emotional "backpacks" are weighted down with several smaller "rocks" of what I'd simply call...

"STUFF"

You know, "stuff" like...

- bitterness
- resentments
- hurts
- grudges
- jealousy
- fears
- unresolved anger
- pettiness
- score-keeping,
- unforgiveness
- helplessness
- "the way it used to be" or "oughta be"
- feelings of worthlessness and
- hopelessness

- self-reliance
- discontent
- weariness and
- worry.

You get the idea.

Years ago I learned about forgiveness the hard way. And since then I've had to re-learn it again and again. I define forgiveness as my giving up the right to hurt you for you hurting me.

It's to be unilateral and unequivocal.

Sometimes people say to me, "Well, you don't know how (fill in the blank) hurt me! If you knew what they did to me, you wouldn't be so quick to talk about forgiveness!" To which I say, "You're right. I don't know what it's like what he / she / they did to you. However, look at a couple of verses with me." And with that I take them to the part of the Lord's Prayer where Jesus says: "For *if you forgive* men when they sin against you, your heavenly Father will also forgive you. But *if you do not* forgive men their sins, your Father will not forgive your sins." [Matthew 6:14-15, NIV, emphasis added.]
Hmm.

Somehow, then, my sense of feeling or being forgiven is directly connected to my (un) willingness to forgive another.

Then I'd have them look with me at where Peter asks Jesus, "'Lord, how many times shall I forgive my brother when he sins against me? Up to seven times?'" [Matthew 18:21, NIV] Now Peter's being generous, as the number seven in the Jewish culture is the number of perfection. However, look at Jesus' response when He says, "I do not say to you, up to seven times, but up to seventy times seven." [Matthew 18:21, NKJV]

That doesn't mean we forgive 490 times, and then on the 491st time we deck 'em!

What Jesus is saying is that forgiveness if a unilateral, ongoing process. In fact, sometimes it's the same event being played over and over again in our minds 490 times! The most powerful point Jesus makes, though, in the remaining verses is that He wants us to see how much we have been forgiven. In the account, "servant A" is us. And God calls us to give an account of our "debt". It's huge; monumental; incalculable.

We cry out for mercy and promise to pay.

(Right.) The king, though (a picture of the Father as Jesus tells us later in v. 35) is moved with compassion and liquidates the debt. We leave happy, happy, happy!

Then we find Servant B who owes us a couple of hundred bucks. We threaten this guy with debtor's prison. He cries out for mercy (just like we did with the king). Only v. 30 says "he (servant A) would not forgive". Not, "he could not" as if he had some other debt he too needed to pay, so this guy can help him get caught up. No, he "would not."

Meaning what? Meaning his will is involved. He's intentionally not letting this go.

So, others tell the king what servant A does to servant B; the king calls servant A in on the carpet, calls him a wicked servant, and asks why he wouldn't forgive what servant B did when he (the king) had forgiven him his debt? Servant A then gets thrown into a prison, and he won't come out until he has paid the debt. (This is a bit of a challenge since, as best we know, he isn't earning any income in this prison.)

However the point is simply this even: though servant A is now in prison, he holds the key to his own release. Which is what? The key of forgiveness: of forgiving servant B. And, if he does, then voila! He's out of prison...not a physical one per se, but definitely a mental and emotional one. All because he views the lesser debt (what servant B owes him – and people do "owe" us!) in light of the greater debt (what we, servants A), owe God.

Now, sometimes people say, "Well, I've forgiven so-and-so, but why do I still have this problem...why does it still come back up in my mind"?

Great question! The reason we still struggle with this is because forgiveness isn't just an act, a decision – like a period on a piece of paper. It's also linear, like a line on a piece of paper. In fact, it's more often like three steps forward, two steps back. Or three steps forward, ten steps back! But we keep at it by repeating this action of forgiving someone every time their face – or that memory – comes up.

And remember too that the deeper the hurt, the longer it takes to heal. While a paper cut may heal overnight, recovering from major surgery takes a lot more time. Eventually, though, by forgiving the other person every time we recount the offense, or that memory reasserts itself, the hurt will lessen in time.

And at some point in the future, all you will have is a scar. Which is what? A reminder of what God's grace and mercy did in your life as you forgave others like you've been forgiven by Him.

So, here then is a simple A-B-C approach for us to begin "removing the "rocks" from our mental and emotional "backpacks":

- ACKNOWLEDGE IT

As in saying, "I've got a problem!" Ask forgiveness or apply forgiveness so where or when needed again, see [Matthew 5:24-25; 6:14-15; 18:21-35]

- BEGIN AGAIN

As Solomon puts it, "For though a righteous man falls seven times, he rises again..." [Proverbs 24:16a, NIV] So, if you fall seven times, you get up again. And again. And again.

- CONCENTRATE ON CHRIST

That is, get your eyes off yourself and the other

person or people and onto Jesus, because as the writer of Hebrews tells us, "Keep your eyes on Jesus, who both began and finished this race we're in. Study how he did it. Because he never lost sight of where he was headed – that exhilarating finish in and with God – he could put up with anything along the way: cross, shame, whatever. And now he's there, in the place of honor, right alongside God." [Hebrews 12:2, TM]

You see, this is what the Cross is all about! It's where we come to "drop the stuff" – that is, our sins or burdens, the weights we're carrying around – at the foot of the Cross.

So why not do that! Empty that backpack you're carrying right now, right at the foot of the cross. You see, emptying our mental and emotional "backpacks" of all that God never intended us or wired us to carry will make this "Incredible Journey" more enjoyable, exciting, lighter, and a lot more fun!

THE INCREDIBLE JOURNEY
Mapping The Christian Life
-Chapter 3-
The Bible: Following The Map

Today we've got maps of just about anything to anywhere. There are...

- Google Maps,
- Yahoo Maps,
- Map Quest
- Rand McNally,
- AAA,
- gas station maps, and even
- government agency maps.

The point is, we've got maps detailing...

- cities,
- states,
- nations,
- park trails,
- mountain passes,
- ocean bottoms, the
- lunar surface, and even the
- human genome.

As I said, we've got maps to and for just about everything.

Of course, a map is only as good as the one's making it, and it only helps or benefits those who actually use it. Some years ago my younger brother Bob and uncle Dean took off from Springfield, Missouri to Florida. Bob told me they knew Florida was south, and they were in the Midwest, so they just headed south. No problem, right?

Right.

We've laughed about it since then. They ended up in New Orleans. That's certainly "south" of Springfield, Missouri! And that's when they decided to get a map. As that old Chinese proverb by Lao Tzu puts it, *"If you don't change directions, you might end up where you are headed."* Or perhaps the late, great "theologian" Yogi Berra put it even better when he said, *"If you don't know where you're going, you might not get there."*

Well, it isn't too difficult for us to draw the parallel between the value of a map or guide book on a long journey, and the value of God's Word [Bible] as The Guide Book or Map for believers on this Incredible Journey known as the Christian life.

Now, to be sure, though, the overwhelming majority of Americans value the Bible. In fact, 9-out-of-10 homes have one. While growing up in Boston we had a big, huge family Bible. We never actually read it. It was more like an ornament; a place where I thought we kept the "family tree"!

In addition, it's the top-selling book in America, with something like $650+/- million sales each year. And when asked what the most influential book is in American history, 4-out-of-5 adults name the Bible. Even the late Peter Jennings of The American Agenda – with its then-12 million viewers – noted a growing trend in the American workplace where *"They are using the Bible as a guide to business."*

However, if the Bible is only seen as a "Guide Book" or a set of directions for "right living", then our Christian life will still feel shallow and hollow. God's deepest desire is for an intimate relationship with us; something more than just memorizing some, or several, of our favorite verses.

Have you ever received a love letter from someone? Well, would you have been content to just let it sit on the table, unread? Hardly! And yet God's Word is like a "love letter" sent to us to convey His love for us. Sadly, research seems to indicate that only 4-out-of-10 actually read the Bible in a typical week, apart from when we're in church. And it's even suggested that fewer than 10% of church-going Christians and important life decisions based on God's Word and seeking His will.

So, for the balance of this chapter, let's take a few moments to see why following this "Map" [this "Guide Book"] is so invaluable and essential for those wanting the best trip possible on this Incredible Journey.

And to help us in this regard, let's use the word "guide" as an acrostic or acronym to identify at least five key elements that we'd expect from a good map. For instance, we'd expect or need a map to be [for the letter "G" of "guide"] in...

GOOD CONDITION

Now, by being in "good condition" what I mean is that it needs to be undamaged, readable, or still in one piece. Obviously if certain parts of a map are missing, then we'd be clueless about a number of things, like:

- what road we're on,
- which detours to take,
- the mileage distance between cities,
- what else there might be to know, see or do.

Allow me to illustrate.

If we held up a filling station map of the continental United States and cut off, say, everything north, south of, and including Missouri, that would leave us hopelessly lost and confused as to what takes place where once we passed, say, Illinois.

The same is with the Bible.

If we leave off 39 books – the Old Testament – and only keep or read 27– the New Testament – there's a lot we wouldn't know. A map in "good condition", then, is absolutely essential and critical if we're to make informed choices, decisions or are in need of directions.

So again, in similar fashion, there's value to us in having and studying both the Old Testament with the New Testament. After all, as another has well said, *"The New is* contained *in the Old, and the Old is* explained *in the New!"* [Just check out the book of Hebrews to see what this means]

And, as the Apostle Paul tells us, "All Scripture is God-breathed and is useful for teaching, rebuking, correcting and training in righteousness..." [2 Timothy 3:16, NIV] This would be a reference to both the Old Testament – already written in Paul's day – and the New Testament – being written in Paul's day [cf., 2 Peter 3:15-16].

And it also helps to explain what Paul's referring to when he says that he had "Not hesitated to proclaim ...the whole will [KJV, "counsel"] of God." [Acts 20:27, NIV] He makes a similar statement later when he appeals to us to "stand firm in all the will of God, mature and fully assured." [Colossians 4:12, NIV]

You see, if we choose to begin and continue on this Incredible Journey, then we need to know that we have, and are in possession of, a "map" that's in "good condition"!

However, our "Guide Book" or map also needs to be [for the letter "U" of "guide"]...

UNDERSTANDABLE

Now, like many of you, I've had the privilege of traveling outside the United States. I've been to such places as...

- Canada [where they speak French],
- Netherlands [Dutch],
- Israel [Hebrew], then
- Greece [Greek],
- Korea [Korean],
- Japan [Japanese], along with
- Mexico,
  Guatemala,
  Nicaragua,
  Costa Rica, and
  Venezuela [Spanish].

And while I know a little "see Spot run" Spanish, I can assure you that even when you know a little of that (or any) language, you'll still need a map that you can read and understand if you plan on going anywhere.

Now, admittedly, some "maps" [Bibles] are hard to understand, especially if they're written in a language we don't speak [i.e., the Old Testament is primarily written in Hebrew; the New Testament in Greek]. For my part, after coming to faith as a teenager, I "cut my teeth" on the

1611 King James Version; however, its 17th century English is hard to understand to 21st century believers.

And besides that, language changes. For instance, take where Peter says, "Likewise, ye wives, be in subjection to your own husbands; that, if any obey not the word, they also may without the word be won by the *conversation* of the wives." [1 Peter 3:1, KJV, emphasis added.]

OK, so what does the word "conversation" mean to you? Talking as in back and forth between or among people is a dialogue between individuals. Of course that's what it means...to us. However, consider how the NIV renders the same verse: "Wives, in the same way be submissive to your husbands so that, if any of them do not believe the word, they may be won over without words by the *behavior* of their wives." [Emphasis added.]

The point? *"Conversation"* in 1611 meant behavior, not talking; in the 21st century it means talking, not behavior.

By the way, for those who fiercely hold to an "only the KJV" translation, I'd like to ask this question: what did believers read prior to 1611?

Or what else came along after that? Different translations are developed to keep up with the changes in grammar. Sometimes they've even created when research or documents surface that shed more insight into a text.

However, to better answer this issue, simply contact the American Bible Society for their Chart of the English Bible. Their address is: American Bible Society, 1865 Broadway, New York, NY 10023. Like an "understandable" map, what you'll receive from them will be most enlightening!

The point is that legitimate, scholarly, and biblically-balanced translations seek to find words in the current culture that most accurately reflect what the Hebrew of the Old and Greek of the New Testament are saying.

So, whether we're new to The Journey or have been on it for sometime, if you're considering a new Bible, you might want to check out a Life Application NIV or NLT.

There are others, of course; however, I've found these to have excellent footnotes. And to me, footnotes are like floodlights on a house; they illuminate the text, or what you're reading. The benefit of these footnotes is that when you're reading a verse and haven't got a clue what it's saying, read below to see if it sheds some "light" on the subject!

Of course, our understanding the "Map" or Guide Book is not only our need as Christ-followers; it's also essential if we're Bible or "Map" teachers; we too need to make it understandable.

And this is precisely what we see happening when we read that "They [the spiritual leaders] read from the Book of the Law of God, making it clear and giving the meaning so that the people could understand what was being read." [Nehemiah 8:8, NIV]

Now, there are those, of course, who say they don't or can't understand the Bible, when what they really mean is that they think this "map" or Guide Book is "too old", ancient history, "boring", and / or irrelevant. That it's just a bunch of...

- rules and regulations,
- old wives tales,
- myths,
- saga,
- legends,
- fables,

- fiction, and
- fairy tales; that it's
- filled with contradictions,
- inaccuracies, is
- outdated, and, you know,
- not scientific.

You get the idea. Some people don't think very highly of the Bible.

At this point you might want to check out Josh McDowell's book, *The New Evidence that Demands a Verdict* (Nashville: Thomas Nelson Publishers, 1999). Or *When Skeptics Ask: A Handbook on Christian Evidences* by Norman Geisler and Ronald Brooks (Grand Rapids: Baker Books, 1990).

Also, anything written by former atheist Lee Strobel is incredibly helpful as well.

Now, on the "lighter side", I did come across a story about an American businessman who happened upon a native in Africa studying his Bible [the "Map"]. And yet, with an air of condescension and undisguised arrogance, the American said, *"In my country that book is old-fashioned and out-of-date."* To which the African, scarcely looking up from his Bible, said with a smile, *"If that Book were out-of-date here you would have been eaten by now."*

Ah, yes!

Well, along with our "map" needing to be in "Good condition" and "Understandable", a third quality we'd expect with a map or our Guide Book is that it be [for the letter "I" of "guide"]...

INFORMATIVE

In other words, we need a map or Guide Book that actually helps benefits or informs us. So, what sorts of benefits come with God's "Map" or "Guide Book"? Well, by it God provides us with...

- wisdom [Psalm 19:7; James 1:5],
- success [Joshua 1:8],
- purity [Psalm 119:9],
- faith [Romans 10:17],
- satisfaction [Psalm 119:92-93], and
- direction [Psalm 119:105].

This is why God's Word is likened to a...

- lamp [Psalm 109:105],
- fire [Jeremiah 23:29],

- hammer [Jeremiah 23:29],
- seed [Mark 4:1-20],
- sword [Ephesians 6:17],
- milk [1 Peter 2:2],
- meat [Hebrews 5:12-14], and a
- scalpel [Hebrews 4:12].

God's Word – this "Map" or "Guide Book" – reveals that there is meaning and purpose to our lives and existence, not meaninglessness, emptiness and hopelessness.

And yet, a good map or Guide Book also alerts us to [for letter "D" of "guide"]...

DANGERS

Consider, for instance, Solomon's warning where he says that "Stern discipline awaits him [her] who leaves the path." [Proverbs 15:10, NIV] He should know; it's what – at the end of his life – he learned the hard way. I mean, even his dad, David, said that "They warn us away from harm and give success to those who obey them." [Psalm 19:11, LB] And he, too, learned this lesson the hard way.

You see, this "Map" or "Guide Book" warns us about all kinds of dangers related to issues that affect and influence our...

- morality [Proverbs 4-7],
- ethics [Proverbs 11:1],
- legal issues [Proverbs 11:15],
- relationships [Proverbs 22:24-25],
- finances [Proverbs 28:22], and
- spirituality [Proverbs 16:18].

Most of us would want to know what and where the dangers are in these areas.

And yet, to deal with dangers related to these areas, we need to have a firm "grasp" of the "Map"; to have a grip on the Word! This is why we're told to...

- hear it [Mark 4:18],
- read it [1 Timothy 4:17],
- study it [2 Timothy 2:15]
- memorize it [Psalm 119:11]
- meditate on it [Joshua 1:8], and then
- apply it [John 13:17]; that is, apply what we know!

And yet, along with this "Map" or "Guide Book" being all that we've seen so far, it also needs to be [for the 5th and final letter "E" of "guide"]...

EXACT

Some time back I received a call from a dear friend who'd just returned from a 6-month tour in Iraq as a Geospatial Intel Analyst. His job entails studying the earth's surface and providing evasion charts for downed pilots. In point of fact, what you handled as it was being passed around earlier is actually a pilot's survival tool! It reveals...

- good and bad plants,
- poisonous and nonpoisonous snakes,
- catch rain water,
- shows where the "safe ground-zone" is from the enemy, and
- It's virtually indestructible.

This, too, is a map that's in...

- "good condition",
- understandable,
- informative, exposing
- dangers, and is
- exact, as in
- precise,
- accurate,
- factual,

- truthful, and
- reflects reality.

In fact, the pilot's life literally depends on it.

And yet, if you're a non-military person, if when you saw this map, most likely you would have had no awareness of the value or importance of the map you were holding. And so it is with many of us who hold the Bible in our hands. We often are clueless of how dependent we are on its contents for our survival.

So, what kind of "Map" or Guide Book do we have? Well, as Proverbs tells us, "Every word of God is flawless; he is a shield to those who take refuge in him. Do not add to his words, or he will rebuke you and prove you a liar." [Proverbs 30:5, NIV]

And as Paul reminds us, "All Scripture is inspired by God and is useful for teaching the faith and correcting error, for resetting the direction of a man's life and training him in good living." [2 Timothy 3:16, Modern English] And Jesus even asks the Father, "Make them holy by the truth; for your word is the truth." [John 17:17, Modern English] And He also says earlier, "You will know the truth and the truth will set you free." [John 8:32, NIV]

Of course, it may make us miserable before it makes us free!

However, as one author notes, fully two-thirds of Americans say that there isn't any such thing as truth or absolute truth. Further, *"many people consider it arrogant, narrow-minded ["insufferable presumption"] and bigoted for Christians to contend that the only path to God must go through Jesus of Nazareth. In a day of religious pluralism and tolerance, this exclusivity claim is politically incorrect, a verbal slap in the face of other belief systems. [One response] labeled it 'absurd religious chauvinism' while [still another] called it a 'spiritual dictatorship,' that fosters the kind of smug and superior attitude that can lead to hatred and violence toward people who believe differently."*

And yet, as Ravi Zacharias [former Hindu-turned-Christian] puts it, *"Every religion at its core is exclusive."*

And there are countless examples we could point to:

- Muslims and Islam are exclusive regarding the Koran and Mohammed;
- Buddhism is exclusive regarding its rejection of Hinduism, and;
- Hinduism is exclusive with regarding to its scriptures, the law of karma and reincarnation;
- Sikhism challenged Buddhism and Hinduism, and;
- atheists or atheism are exclusive regarding the rejection of God, and;
- Baha'ism excludes the exclusivists!

So, what it all comes down to is what we believe or do about "The Map Maker" [Jesus]. And, as Jesus Himself tells us, "Heaven and earth will pass away, but My words will not pass away." [Matthew 24:35, NAB] So, what *do* you think about Jesus?!

I love how C.S. Lewis puts it: *"I am trying here to prevent anyone saying the really foolish thing that people often say about Him: 'I'm ready to accept Jesus as a great moral teacher, but I don't accept His claim to be God.' That is the one thing we must not say. A man who was merely a man and said the sort of things Jesus said would not be a great moral teacher. He would either be a lunatic – on a*

*level with the man who says he is poached egg –
or else he would be the Devil of Hell. You must
make your choice. Either this man was and is, the
son of God; or else a madman or something
worse."*

Then Lewis adds, *"You can shut Him up for a fool,
you can spit at Him and kill Him as a demon; or
you can fall at His feet and call Him Lord and God.
But let us not come up with any patronizing
nonsense about His being a great human teacher.
He has not left that open to us. He did not intend
to."*

This "Map"; this "Guide Book" – is eternal! In
fact, as many commonly refer to the Bible, what
it really means is *Basic Instructions Before
Leaving Earth*!

This is why this Guide Book, this Map, is so
invaluable to have and follow on this Incredible
Journey known as the Christian life. Not as an
end in itself, not as a destination; rather, it's a
Map we can follow and learn from in order to
cultivate this growing, personal relationship
with our Lord and Savior, Jesus Christ.

THE INCREDIBLE JOURNEY
Mapping The Christian Life
-Chapter 4-
The Spirit: Connecting with Our Guide

At this point I hope we're beginning to see that the Christian life is far more than merely...

- believing the "right things",
- practicing the "right behaviors",
- going through the "right motions",
- keeping the "right rules or rituals", or even
- being a member of the "right church" – whatever that's supposed to mean.

And that it's really more than our simply or only...

- Knowing God [Chapter 1],
- Dealing with our Past [Chapter 2], and
- Following the "Map" [Chapter 3].

True, all of these are essential, even critical. However, it's more than a code of ethics, a list of doctrines, or even steps to take to improve our marriage, families or finances. It's about "going deeper and growing stronger" in our love and passion for its Author. This chapter entitled

"Connecting with our Guide" deals with the Holy Spirit's role in our lives – and it's going to look at the one topic that is probably the least understood – or perhaps the most misunderstood – subject related to the Christian life.

Now, although Holy Spirit is mentioned some 88 times in the Old Testament and some 262 times the New Testament, He still comes across as something of the "Silent Partner" of the Trinity. I mean, the Father and Son [Jesus] we get, we understand; but the "Holy Spirit" [KJV, "Ghost"]?! Hmmm!

While serving as pastor in Hawaii and teaching as an adjunct faculty member for one of the satellite campuses of Wayland Baptist University I had one student who expressed his skepticism about Christians worshipping *one* God. He stated that Christians actually worship *three* (3) gods: the Father [God]; Jesus [who is God], and; the Spirit [also God].

That, to him, plainly means Christians are not *mono*theists – worshiping one God – but polytheists – worshiping many gods.

I suggested that an analogy might be helpful at

this point.

Consider water. It's found in three (3) forms: liquid, solid (ice) and as a gas (or vapor; steam). At that point, however, I added that any analogy tends to break down as they can't be all three at one time. At that point a student at the back of the room raised his hand and said, *"Dr. Martin, I'm a physics major. In the realm of physics water does exist in three forms simultaneously. It's called the 'triple point of water.'"* To which I then said, *"Why thank you! You just helped to make my point!"*

Well, let's see if we can get a handle or understanding as to who or what the Spirit is by using a series of what I'd simply call "interview questions". These are the sort of questions one might typically ask a tour guide on a journey. They're actually the sort of questions I asked our guides when we toured Mt. Rushmore, Little Big Horn, the Crazy Horse Memorial, Israel, and even Kilwin's Chocolate Factory in upper Michigan!

For instance, we'd probably begin by asking our Guide – whom we already know or call the Holy Spirit –an introductory sort of question, like:

"DO YOU GO BY OTHER NAMES?"

Now, guides often wear a badge or name tag, so this seems to be a normal starting point or place to begin with a human tour guide. In fact, I suspect that some of us have or have gone by different names. People often ask me, *"What do we call you?"* Is it...

- Dave or David?
- James or James David?
- Pastor?
- Bro. Dave or Pastor Dave? Or
- Preacher or "Preacher-man"?
- Dr. Martin or Dr. Dave?
- Doc Martin,
- Reverend Martin,
- "Soul Dr.", or
- "Hey you!"?

In fact, how many of us actually have a nickname or pet name? [Never mind! I don't want to go there!]

The point is that the Holy Spirit does have a number of names [20+], among them being:

- The Spirit of God [Matthew 3:16],
- The Spirit of Christ [Romans 8:9],

61

- The Sprit of Holiness [Romans 1:4],
- The Spirit of Wisdom [Ephesians 1:17],
- The Spirit of Faith [2 Corinthians 4:13], and
- The Spirit of Adoption [Romans 8:15].

He also goes by the names Helper and / or Comforter. And why do you suppose that is? Because most if not all of us, at some time or another, are going to be some help and comfort.

Well, after learning any other names our Guide goes by, perhaps a second question we might want to ask is:

"WHAT ELSE DO YOU DO?"

I mean, is this a full-time job, or do you do something else on the side? Of course, in the Spirit's case, we discover that, among other things, He...

- convicts us of sin / guilt
[As John 16:8 indicates, He serves as the "Prosecuting Attorney" of the Trinity]; He:
- "births" us into the body of Christ [John 3:5]; He:
- "fills us" [Ephesians 5:18]

This is a qualitative term, not a quantitative one. It's not as if we're "full of the Spirit" or only "half full". It refers to the quality of our life that results from the Spirit "filling" us. He:

- produces "fruit" in us [Galatians 5:22-23]

This is the evidence of being "filled": "love, joy, peace, patience, kindness, goodness, faithfulness, gentleness, and self-control. Here there is no conflict with the law." He:

- "gifts" us [1 Corinthians 12:11], and; He
- empowers us [Acts 1:8]

It's as if He's the engine under the hood! Beyond this, He:

- seals us [Ephesians 1:13-14],
- indwells us [1 Corinthian 6:19-20],
- assures us [Romans 8:16],
- strengthens us [Ephesians 3:16],
- hears us [John 16:13],
- leads / guides us [Romans 8:14], and He
- "speaks" to us [in that "still small voice"; Acts 10:19; 1 Kings 19:12].

And God also uses His Word, people, circumstances, music, books, conferences, etc. to do speak to us. In addition, the Spirit:

- teaches us [John 14:26],
- produces unity [Ephesians 4:3],
- prays for us [Romans 8:26-27],
- forbids certain actions [Acts 16:6-7],
- reveals truth to us [John 16:14],
- reveals God's will to us [1 Corinthians 2:12],
- calls us to serve [Acts 13:2], and He most especially
- exalts Jesus! [1 Corinthians 12:3].

So following such an impressive and exhaustive resume, we might feel prompted to ask our Guide a third question, like:

"HOW LONG HAVE YOU BEEN AT THIS?"

To which we'd hear the Spirit say, *"Forever!" "For eternity" "Before time began and after time ends!"* Why? Because, as the writer of Hebrews puts it, "For by the help of the *eternal* Holy Spirit, Christ willingly gave himself to God to die for our sins." [Hebrews 9:14, LB, emphasis added.]

Of course, He'd probably add the caveat that in Old Testament times He *"came upon people"* [i.e., Gideon, Saul, Samson, etc.], whereas, since

Pentecost [50 days after Jesus crucifixion], He [and the Greek always uses a masculine pronoun in reference to the Spirit] comes to *"live in us!"*

Consider Hebrews 13:5b in the Amplified Version: "For He (God) Himself has said, I will not in any way fail you *nor* give you up *nor* leave you without support. [I will] not, [I will] not, [I will] not in any degree leave you helpless, *nor* forsake *nor* let [you] down, [relax my hold on you], – Assuredly not!"

Here the writer employs a triple negative. Although we typically don't say *"I will* not never (a double negative) *go to the store",* the Greek language does use a double negative to reinforce a point. However, in Hebrews 13:5, the writer's use of a triple negative which is intended to strengthen the point so as to be beyond debate or question; it's iron-clad.

The point? That God will never, ever, under any circumstance leave us nor abandon us. Not now, not later, not in life, not at death, not under any circumstances. As Paul puts it:

"Can *anything ever separate us* from Christ's love? Does it mean he no longer loves us if we have trouble or calamity, or are persecuted, or are hungry or cold or in danger or threatened with death? (Even the Scriptures say, 'For your sake we are killed every day; we are being slaughtered like sheep.') No, despite all these things, overwhelming victory is ours through Christ, who loved us. And I am convinced that *nothing can ever separate us from his love.* Death can't, and life can't. The angels can't, and the demons can't. Our fears for today, our worries about tomorrow, and even the powers of hell can't keep God's love away. Whether we are high above the sky or in the deepest ocean, *nothing in all creation will ever be able to separate us* from the love of God that is revealed in Christ Jesus our Lord." [Romans 8:35-39, NLT, emphasis added.]

And yet, though the Spirit is always "resident", the question we need to answer is this: is He "president"? As in "Is He in charge", "Is He running the show", "calling the shots". You get the idea.

Well, by now we might be tempted to ask a fourth question, like:

"IS THERE ANYTHING YOU DON'T KNOW?"

Or can't do? I mean, our Guide seems to know

everything about this Journey and us – and so we'd hear Him say to this question, "*No*", since, after all, He is:

- Omnipotent

That is, He's all-powerful and can do anything!" For instance, Luke records that "The angel replied, 'The Holy Spirit will come upon you and the power of the Most High will overshadow you. So the baby born to you will be holy and he will be called the Son of God.'" [Luke 1:35, NLT]

The Spirit of God, then, does the sort of things that only God can do: cause a supernatural pregnancy by having the Messiah (Jesus) be born of a virgin. And He's...

- Omnipresent

This simply means that, like gravity and oxygen on Planet Earth, He's the same everywhere at same time. As David records it: "Where can I go *from Your Spirit*? Or where can I flee from Your presence? If I ascend into heaven, You are there; If I make my bed in hell, behold, You are there. If I take the wings of the morning, and dwell in the uttermost parts of the sea, Even there Your hand shall lead me, and Your right hand shall hold me.

" [Psalm139:7-10, NKJV, emphasis added.]

And He's...

- Omniscient

Which simply means He knows everything there is to know, or could be know; all the variables, all the options, all the various scenarios of every event, at any time and for all time. As Paul puts it: "But we know these things because God has revealed them to us by his Spirit and his Spirit searches out everything and shows us even God's deep secrets. No one can know what anyone else is really thinking except that person alone and no one can know God's thoughts except God's own Spirit." [1 Corinthians 2:10-11, NLT]

Now, upon learning all of these incredible truths about our Guide, we may want to ask a fifth question, like:

"DOES ANYTHING EVER REALLY BOTHER YOU?"

You know, like "get under your skin?" "Bug You?" "Upset You?" And at that point we'd hear Him say, *"Yes, whenever we:*

- "grieve" Him   [Ephesians 4:3]

Here the word literally means *"to cause pain or sorrow"*. And what would do this? Sin. And note, too, that the Spirit is not a *"force"* as you can't "grieve" a force; or

- "quench" Him   [1 Thessalonians 5:19]

Here the word literally means *"to douse, pour water on"*. And what would do this- Legalism, formalism, carnality, being judgmental, a critical spirit, disunity, etc. Or;

- "resist" Him [Acts 7:51]

And here the word literally means *"to oppose"* [as with regard to His will]; or, we try to

- lie to / deceive Him [Acts 5:3]

Which is a bit difficult to imagine since (as God) He knows all there is to know! So who do we think we're kidding? Or we can:

- rebel against Him [Isaiah 63:10].

That is, we simply decide we aren't going to do what He wants! We're going to do our will, our way, in our own sweet time. Well, that's going to lead us into some pretty deep weeds.

So by now we'd probably be so impressed by our Heavenly Guide – with who He is, how much He knows and does, and how He relates to us – that perhaps a sixth and final question might be:

"WILL YOU BE WITH US THE WHOLE JOURNEY?"

From beginning to end, start to finish? To which His reply will be a resounding *"Yes!"* For as Paul tells us: "And you also were included in Christ when you heard the word of truth, the gospel of your salvation. Having believed, you were marked in him with a seal, the promised Holy Spirit, who is a deposit guaranteeing our inheritance   until the redemption of those who are God's possession – to the praise of his glory."[Ephesians 1:13-14, NLT]

Or as The Message paraphrases those verses,

"It's in Christ that you, once you heard the truth and believed it (this Message of your salvation), found yourselves home free – signed, sealed and delivered by the Holy Spirit. This signet from God is the first installment on what's coming, a reminder that we'll get everything God has planned for us, a praising and glorious life."

So, how does any of this begin or become a reality for us? What we as believers / Christians need to do is fairly simple:

1. Repent of, confess, or come clean about any known sin [1 John 1:9. Why? Because He won't *"fill"* a dirty vessel!]

2. Daily ask the Spirit to *"fill"* or *"control"* you [Ephesians 5:18; LB, "be filled...with the Spirit, and controlled by him"], then;

3. Believe by faith [not your feelings!] that He *has* filled you and *is* filling you!

For as John tells us, "And we are sure of this, that he will listen to us whenever we ask him for anything in line with his will. And if we really know he is listening when we talk to him and make our requests, then we can be sure that he will answer us." [1 John 5:14, LB]

And lastly:

4. Surrender yourself and your will to Him and His control – daily.

This is why Paul says of himself that "I die daily..." [1 Corinthians 15:31, KJV] And why he adds that "I myself no longer live, but Christ lives in me. So I live my life in this earthly body by trusting in the Son of God, who loved me and gave himself for me." [Galatians 2:20, NLT]

So, on a practical level, now is the time for us to – in the words of a song by Chris Tomlin – *"raise the white flag"* of full surrender to our Heavenly Guide, the Holy Spirit!

THE INCREDIBLE JOURNEY
Mapping The Christian Life
-Chapter 5-
Fellowship: The Value of Hiking Partners

Let's begin with a little word association. What comes to mind when you hear the word "fellowship"?

Well, for a lot of people – especially Baptists! – we either think of food, a place [as in a fellowship hall], or an event, [ice cream fellowship]. Now, while all of these terms are often associated with the word "fellowship", none of them have anything to do with what the biblical term actually means. As when Luke records that *"They continued steadily learning the teaching of the apostles and joined in the fellowship."* [Acts 2:42, Modern English, emphasis added.] Because here the Greek word for *"fellowship"* is *"koinonia"*, which literally means *"a sharing in common"*, as in true community, *"the common life"*, or *"doing life together"*!

And while those words may involve food, places and events – even friendships and relationships – the word actually means a great deal more. Allow me to give you an illustration.

Consider a bag of marbles. They're certainly in a "group"; however, they're hard, and they ricochet off each other. I've found some churches and their members to be like that, haven't you? They never connect; once you walk through the church doors, you almost feel like you're imposing, just by showing up.

Then there are tennis balls. They're lined up in the tube and are warm and fuzzy. However, when they're "let out of the tube" [i.e., the pews; a church building], they go their separate ways.

Again, when it comes to some churches I've been to, "been there, done that."

Then there are grapes. Ah, they're connected, like life on a vine – and in time and over time they "bleed" together. They're the "real deal", as opposed to plastic, decorative grapes that look real but are fake, phony and artificial. And some churches...well, you know what I mean.

So in this chapter we'll look at The Value of Hiking Partners [fellowship], because, while there may be and are times when we enjoy and need some privacy or time alone, a journey like this without a hiking partner could prove to be dangerous and even fatal to our spiritual life.

Short of that, it's certainly a lot more fun and enjoyable if we have someone to experience this Journey with us!

Now, on at least two occasions, though, I learned first hand the value of having and being a hiking partner. The first time was when our daughter Jayne and I climbed Horn Peak which is located in the Sangre de Cristo range of the Rockies. Not that hiking this mountain range is like tackling the Matterhorn or the mountains depicted in movies like *Vertical Limit* or *Mission Impossible II!* While climbing Horn Peak is challenging, it certainly isn't terrifying. And yet, the Big Horn rises to 13,450, while the Little Horn stops at 13,143, with the tree line being at 11,000 feet, and the hike is a 10-mile round trip.

In any case, the first part of the hike or journey isn't all that bad. When I began I had visions of Julie Andrews and *The Sound of Music*...just sort of traipsing along meadows as we climbed the mountain.

Right!

It was when we began our ascent of Little Horn that our daughter needed some of water...and I had the canteen! So, to entice, encourage and motivate her to keep pressing on, I'd position myself ahead and above her, wave and shake the canteen to bait her so as to keep her moving. [I know, I know...you're thinkin' "What kinda dad are you, anyway?!]

Well, there's a method to the madness, so stick with me here and you'll see why.

Once she reached me we'd rest, eat a snack, talk, take in the view, drink some water, and then continue our climb to the Big Horn. And then, on our way down the mountain I asked her what it was that motivated her; you know, kept her going and not give up. I was hoping she'd say something like, "To be like you, O mighty climber!"

Uh-uh.

Her response was: "To prove to you that I could!" Yep! There, you've got it. Spoken like the true Type-A, persevering, determined take-the-mountain gal she is!

The second occasion where I experienced the value of a hiking partner was a bit scarier. This time it involved our son David and nephew

Jamie. Same mountain, same trip. They'd made it to the top before us, and on their way down our nephew lost his balance by pitching forward. He fell face forward into the rocks, and started rolling head-over-heels down the slope.

I tried to move sideways to stop his fall; however, the rocks did that for me. Other hikers ran back to camp, and the campsite sent a guide on horseback to carry our nephew back to the lodge and into town where a local doctor put a dozen stitches in his head.

In both cases, however, having or being a hiking partner proved to be both invaluable and essentially, even life-saving.

So, by way of parallel, there's value in our having or being a "hiking partner" when it comes to our living out this experience called the Christian life.

Now, to help us see and appreciate this value, this time let's use the word "partner" as an acronym or acrostic to identify some of the key traits or qualities necessary for this relationship. And perhaps the initial and most appropriate trait or quality needed for our journey is identified with or by the letter "P" [of partner] signifying someone who's...

PERSEVERING

In other words, when it comes to our spiritual journey, we need – and need to be – hiking partners with grit, determination, and stamina; someone who's willing to...

- go the distance,
- endure,
- not give up,
- throw in the towel,
- quit, or
- turn back.

You see, the hardest part of any hike – like it often is with some remodeling project – is when we hit mid-way, mid-stream, or mid-point – when we're halfway there...and we just want to quit. And quite frankly, this particular trait or quality is absolutely essential for any kind of partner or partnership – be it a...

- hiking partner,
- business partner,
- golfing partner,
- work-out partner, or
- marriage partner.

Small wonder why Solomon tells us that "If you falter in times of trouble, how small is your strength." [Proverbs 24:10, NIV] Or, as God Himself says that "If racing with mere men... has wearied you, how will you race against horses....If you stumble and fall on open ground, what will you do in [the] jungles?" [Jeremiah 12:5, LB] Meaning if you think whatever you're going through is so bad, just imagine what it'll be like when you have some real problems!

And this is also why the writer of Hebrews tells us to: "Think of what [Jesus] went through, how he put up with so much hatred from sinful men! So do not let yourselves become discouraged and give up. For in your struggle against sin you have not yet had to fight to the point of being killed." [Hebrews 12:3-4, TEV]

So, a "hiking partner" on this Incredible Journey, then, helps to motivate us to "keep on keepin' on." And yet, along with "Persevering", the "A" trait for a "partner" could stand for or represent someone who's...

ACCEPTING

Now, by "accepting" I mean someone who's accepting another's...

- help / advice [like other "hikers", or from our "Guide", or from the "Map"]; or
- another's point of view,
- perspective,
- expertise, or even
- accepting adverse circumstances, difficulties, challenges, or the

- mistakes, foibles, quirks, mishaps of other "hikers" on the journey.

Sometimes people say to me, *"Well, I know I'm not perfect!"* To which I'll say, *"Then why are you expecting your husband/wife/child(ren), parent(s) to be perfect?!"* I mean, none of us are perfect, none of us have "arrived", and none of us have all the answers. So there's always something of value that another "hiking partner" has to offer.

Which I think helps to explain why Paul tells us to "Accept one another as Christ accepted us ..." [Romans 15:7, Modern English] And then later, when it comes to accepting difficulties, Paul even adds that we should "Give thanks in all circumstances, for this is the will of God in Christ Jesus for you." [1 Thessalonians 5:18, RSV]

And yet, along with persevering and accepting,

we also need "hiking partners" that are [for the letter R of partner]:

RELIABLE

You know, trustworthy, dependable, able to "pull their own weight" when it comes to traveling this journey. Because as Solomon puts it. "Putting confidence in an unreliable man [woman] is like chewing with a sore tooth, or trying to run on a broken foot." [Proverbs 25:19, LB]

It was pollster George Barna [of the Barna Research Group] in his book *The Power of Team Leadership*, who once said: *"...a...team [must] be comprised of individuals who are willing to work hard at making the team a healthy unit....This invariably requires a willingness to sacrifice personal rewards and resources for the good of the team.....Teams also need partners who respect and believe in one another....It is difficult to pursue risks if you do not trust the motives or abilities of others to make appropriate choices or to provide support. If a deep   level of trust does not exist, team members are not likely to rely upon one another's judgment or capabilities when key moments arise....If one member slacks off, the entire team suffer."*

The point? It takes a team mentality for individual "hikers", as well as a church, to thrive.

However, along with needing "hiking partners" who are persevering, accepting and reliable, they and we also need [for the letter "T" of partner] to be...

TRUTHFUL

For instance, if or when you're climbing a mountain and you or your hiking partner spots danger, that's when you need someone to tell you – or for you to tell – the truth.

While hiking with Dick and Sue Vanderlinde, some dear "friends for the journey", in some mountains near their home in Albuquerque, New Mexico, Dick warned me about what I'd encounter after making a sharp turn to the left on a mountain: a path about a foot wide, with a wind hitting the mountainside that could, if I wasn't careful, knock me off balance and off the mountain.

In other words, if I wanted to get to the other side, I'd have to hug the mountain! "Got it!" I said. And sure enough, when I made the sharp left turn, the wind blasted me against the wall of the mountainside. Sure glad Dick told me the truth about what to expect!

And yet, if someone sees or knows the danger and yet fails to give us a warning, to tell us the truth about what we're facing, that would make them what? At best, irresponsible and lacking a former trait, making them *un*reliable. This is why, when it comes to how we relate to potential "hikers" we're given such an incredibly strong and somber warning by God Himself when He says: "So listen to what I say and warn them for me. When I say to the wicked, 'O wicked man, you will die!' and you don't tell him what I say, so that he does not repent – that wicked person will die in his sins, but I will hold you responsible for his death. But if you warn him to repent and he doesn't, he will die in his sin and you will not be responsible." [Ezekiel 33:7-9, LB]

There's even a New Testament parallel where Jude says: "Try to help those who argue against you. Be merciful to those who doubt. Save some by snatching them as from the very flames of hell itself. And as for others, help them to find the Lord by being kind to them, but be careful that you yourselves aren't pulled along into their sins. Hate every trace of their sin while being merciful to them as sinners." [Jude 1:22-23, LB]

In other words, "hate the sin, but love the sinner!" And yet, there may be times when we or others don't...

- want the truth,
- like the truth, be
- be told the truth,
- hear the truth, or even
- heed the truth.

Several years ago I sensed a prompting by God's Spirit to approach a young lady from our church. She was working in a mall near our home, and she was becoming seriously involved with a young man who had major problems. I drove to the mall, praying like crazy that God would give me the words to say. This was a bit out of my comfort zone, and yet I sensed that I was to appeal to her to break off this relationship.

When I got to the store where she worked I saw her standing toward the front; however, as I approached her the boyfriend suddenly appeared from the right of me. "Uh-oh!" I thought. "This is gonna get tricky!"

Sure enough, when I called out her name, she turned, and he immediately stood by her. As politely as I knew how, and *"speaking the truth in love"* [Ephesians 4:15] I made the appeal to her to break off this relationship; that God had actually sent me to tell her that. [I thought those words might bolster my argument, if not my confidence. Regarding the latter, it didn't, but I said them anyway.]

Well, she – and he – read me the "riot act": "Who do you think you are..." etc., etc., etc. Well, as you might suspect, it got ugly, at least from their response. I simply repeated my appeal and then turned to leave. And, as I walked away, they continued to hurl their invectives at me.

Well, naturally I felt horrible! I was sick to my stomach. This was not at all a pleasant experience. I'm not quite sure what I expected, but this wasn't it. And yet, at the same time, I did what I thought God was requiring of me: to try and rescue someone from a self-destructive path.

I later learned that she moved to Florida to live with her boyfriend.

About a year later my secretary told me that

"someone was in the office to see me." When I inquired as to who it was, she related this girl's name to me. I immediately opened my door to welcome her in. She began weeping as she sat down in my office. She then poured out all of the hurt and heartache she'd experienced that year, and said she so regretted not following my appeal the year before. We prayed. We hugged. And we welcomed her back into the family of believers. Yay, God!

What we need are "hiking partners" who love us enough, and care about us enough, to hold us accountable and tell us the truth. As Proverbs tells us, "Wounds from a friend are better than kisses from an enemy!" [Proverbs 27:6, LB]

And along with needing "hiking partners" who are persevering, accepting, reliable and truthful, they and we also need to be...

NEARBY

In other words, close at hand, accessible [like grapes], not "off by themselves" so we have to fend for ourselves. This is part of the reason why the writer of Hebrews tells us to "not neglect our church meetings, as some people do, but encourage and warn each other, especially now that they day of his coming back again is drawing near." [Hebrews 10:25, LB]

You see, being involved and getting connected to a body of believers – whether in a Life Group, worship or ministry team, etc. – is actually God's way of providing us with a sort of built-in-support group. Biblically you see this; where God pairs up people to help, support, and be "near-by" each other. For instance, we find:

- Elijah being linked up with Elisha,
- David depends on his friend Jonathan,
- Peter's connected to John-Mark, and
- Paul's hanging out with Barnabas, Timothy, Titus, Silas, and Luke.

Why, in this vein, we can even see that Jesus doesn't "go it alone" – in a manner of speaking, He too has twelve "hiking partners" with Him. Small wonder why Solomon tells us that: "You are better off to have a friend than to be all alone....If you fall, your friend can help you up. But if you fall without having a friend nearby, you are really in trouble." [Ecclesiastes 4:9-10, CEV]

So, Samuel Taylor Coleridge was right when he wrote that *"Friendship is a sheltering tree."* And yet, we also need "hiking partners" who [for the 7letter "E" of partner] are...

ENCOURAGING

Especially if we're "newbies" or beginners to the Incredible Journey, although I also think "lifers" and "veterans" need doses of encouragement from time-to-time as well. Because as Hebrews puts it, "*Encourage* each other every day while is it 'today.' Help each other so none of you will become hardened because sin has tricked you." [Hebrews 3:13, NCV, emphasis added.] And then later we read, "Think of ways to *encourage* one another to out-burst of love and good deeds." [Hebrews 10:24, NCV, emphasis added.]

Even Paul makes a similar appeal when he writes, "So *encourage* each other to build each other up, just as you are already doing." [NCV, "*Encourage* each other and give each other strength."] [1 Thessalonians 5:11, LB, emphasis added.]

And again, we do this by being in community with one another; talking to and caring for one another. As Leonard Sweet puts it, "*The challenge of the church in the 21st century is to make itself less of an institution and more of a community, less of a place that asks, 'What can you do for us?' and more a place that asks, 'What can we do for you?';...less led by people prone to call a meeting than by people prone to start a conversation. Basically the church has only two things to offer the world: Christ and community."*

Well, for our final letter in "partner" ["R"] we also need "hiking partners" who are...

RESOURCEFUL

Ah, and this means making use of whatever gifts, talents, abilities, strengths, skills we may have and / or could develop. And everybody has something they can do, something they can contribute; we are better together than running "solo". As Paul puts it: "Just as there are many parts to our bodies, so it is with Christ's body. We are all parts of it and it takes every one of us [every "hiking partner"] to make it complete, for we each have different work to do. So we belong to each other and each needs all the others." [Romans 12:4-5, LB]

The point, of course, is that each and every "hiking partner" is uniquely designed, equipped, created and gifted by God for significance and ministry, using what we've got. So, as Peter puts it: "God has given each of you some special abilities; be sure to use them to help each other, passing on to others God's many kinds of blessings." [1 Peter 4:10, LB]

Like our dear "journey-long" friends Sheri [short for Sheridan] and Nancee Dutchik. He's the quiet type; however, when he speaks, people listen. Nancee, on the other hand, likes to say she puts her foot in her mouth so often she has lipstick on her ankles!

But for the many years we journeyed together where I served as pastor (and since then as well), I always counted on Sheri to give me godly counsel for a lot of the tough decisions I faced. And Nancee was always the first to make guests feel welcome into the church. His gift of wisdom and her gift of friendship, and their gift of a servant-spirit made an eternal difference in people's lives. They still do.

It's time for some of us to "step up"; to get connected, get involved: maybe check out a Life Group, or link up with some ministry team, or simply "cross the line of faith" and then follow Jesus in believer's baptism. [Cf., Matt. 28:18-20] Whatever it may be, whatever area it may involve, remember this: that Christ is the Ultimate Hiking Partner.

And, as Solomon reminds us, "There are 'friends' who pretend to be friends, but there is a friend who sticks closer than a brother." [Proverbs 18:24, NLT]

And that's exactly who and what Jesus is to us!

THE INCREDIBILE JOURNEY
Mapping the Christian Life
-Chapter 6-
Worship: The View from a Mountain Top

How many of us have ever had what you might consider a "Mountain Top" experience spiritually-speaking? Yeah! Me too. Maybe it happened at a...

- church service or camp; at
- home or work, a
- revival or crusade,
- retreat or conference,
- concert, or at a
- campground or camp-meeting.

And most often the common denominator in every case is that we met God, or God met us; that He did something in us, to us, for us, or with us. We were somehow changed for the better. It was, in every senses of the word, a worship experience; a summit or high point in our walk with God.

Well, with this chapter, we've arrived at the summit on our Incredible Journey! Now it's about Worship: the View from a Mountain Top.

And if there was ever a "Mountain Top" worship experience-encounter with God, it's found in 1 Kings 19. And beginning with vv. 8-13 [LB] we read that "He [Elijah] got up and ate and drank, and the food gave him enough strength to travel forty days and forty nights to Mt. Horeb, the mountain of God, where he lived in a cave. But the Lord said to him, 'What are you doing here, Elijah?' He replied, 'I have worked very hard for the Lord God of the heavens; but the people of Israel have broken their covenant with you and torn down your altars and killed your prophets and only I am left and now they are trying to kill me too.' 'Go out and stand before me on the mountain,' the Lord told him. And as Elijah stood there the Lord passed by and a mighty windstorm hit the mountain; it was such a terrible blast that the rocks were torn loose, but the Lord was not in the wind. After the wind, there was an earthquake, but the Lord was not in the earthquake. And after the earthquake, there was a fire, but the Lord was not in the fire. And after the fire, there was the sound of a gentle whisper. [KJV, "a still small voice"] When Elijah heard it, he wrapped his face in his scarf and went out and stood at the entrance of the cave. And a voice said, 'Why are you here, Elijah?'"

Well, Elijah's certainly having a "Mountain Top" worship encounter with God.

And then there's Moses' experience where we read: "And the Lord said to Moses, 'Come up to me on the mountain. Stay there while I give you the tablets of stone that I have inscribed with my instructions and commands. Then you will teach the people from them.' So Moses and his assistant Joshua climbed up the mountain of God. Moses told the other leaders, 'Stay here and wait for us until we come back. If there are any problems while I am gone, consult with Aaron and Hur, who are here with you.' Then Moses went up the mountain and the cloud covered it. And the glorious presence of the Lord rested upon Mount Sinai, and the cloud covered it for six days. On the seventh day the Lord called to Moses from the cloud. The Israelites at the foot of the mountain saw an awesome sight. The awesome glory of the Lord on the mountaintop looked like a devouring fire. Then Moses disappeared into the cloud as he climbed higher up the mountain. He stayed on the mountain forty days and forty nights." [Exodus 24:12-18, NLT]

Wow! So Moses, along with some 70 leaders and elders also know what a "Mountain Top" worship experience or encounter with God is like.

And yet, what comes to our mind whenever we hear the word, or think about, worship? Do we associate it with:

- an order of service or liturgy? Or perhaps
- a building and seating?
- Stained glass and candles?
- Kneeling benches and vestments?
- Prayers and offerings?
- Perhaps silence and meditation?
- Certain kinds of music or time / day of the week?
- A praise band, team, choir and orchestra? Or;
- Biblically-based messages that may include communion?

Well, to be sure, any or all of these may be a part of some worship experience.

However, any true, authentic, God-centered "Mountain Top" worship experience is something else and far more than what these external elements indicate or involve. Consider what Jesus tells us: "The time is coming – it has, in fact, come – when what you're called will not matter and where you go to worship will not matter. It's who you are and the way you live that count before God. Your worship must engage your spirit in the pursuit of truth. That's the kind of people the Father is out looking for: those who are simply and honestly themselves before him in their worship. God is sheer being itself – Spirit. Those who worship him must do it out of their very being, their spirits, their true selves, in adoration." [John 4:23-24, TM]

And, as the psalmist adds, "The Lord is pleased only with those who worship him and trust his love." [Psalm 147:11, CEV]   So this is why "Mountain Top" worship experiences are such an integral part of the Christian life, this Incredible Journey!

You see, worship – real, life-changing worship – has as much do with our life as it does with our lips. It's active, not passive – like sitting in church on a Sunday with folded arms and an indifferent, ho-hum attitude that says, "C'mon, move me, preacher!" As devotional writer Oswald Chambers is quoted as saying: *There is only one Being who can satisfy the last aching abyss of the human heart, and that is the Lord Jesus Christ.*"

Our need is to rediscover worship, what's often referred to as the *"missing jewel"* in a Christian's life. Consider the words of another: *"When I was a little girl we used to play church. We'd get the chairs into rows, fight over who'd be the preacher, vigorously lead the hymn singing, and generally have a great carnal time. The aggressive kids naturally wanted to be up front, directing or preaching. The quieter ones were content to sit and be entertained by the up-fronters. Occasionally we'd get mesmerized by a true sensationalistic crowd- swayer like the girl who said, 'Boo! I'm the Holy Ghost!' But in general, if the up-fronters were pretty good they could hold their audience quite a while. If they weren't so good, eventually the kids would drift off to play something else – like jump rope or jacks. Now that generation has grown up, but most of them haven't changed too much. Every Sunday they still play church. They line up in rows for entertainment. If it's pretty good, their church may grow. If it's not too hot, eventually they'll drift off to play something else, like yachting or wife-swapping."*

This is why worship, true worship, is to be real and daily. Here's how Paul puts: "So then, my friends, because of God's great mercy to us I appeal to you: Offer yourselves as a living sacrifice to God, dedicated to his service and pleasing to him. *This is the true worship* [NIV, *"the spiritual act of worship"*] that you should offer. Do not conform yourselves to the standards of this world, but let God transform you inwardly by a complete change of your mind. Then you will be able to know the will of God – what is good and is pleasing to him and is perfect." [Romans 12:1-2, TEV, emphasis added.]

So, as the psalmist tells us, "Worship him continually." [Psalm 105:4, TEV]

From God's vantage-point worship is to be seen as a fundamental, foundational, non-negotiable to our spiritual journey. It often marks – or should mark – those "summit point" times in our lives.

Well, then, how will we know – what does it take – to reach, have, and / or experience these summit-like moments? Will it only be when we have goose bumps, tears, and an emotional rush? Maybe… maybe not. What we do know is that, as James tells us, "We please God by what we *do* and not only by what we believe". [James 2:24, CEV, emphasis added.]

So let's consider a familiar conversation that

Jesus has with a religious leader in Mark 12:28-30 [NCV]. There it records that "One of the teachers of the law came and heard Jesus arguing with the Sadducees."

Sadducees? Who are they? Well, an explanation may be in order here. In current parlance, these are what we'd call left-wing, religious liberals. In Century One they're smaller in number than the Pharisees. The Pharisees, on the other hand, make up what we'd call the right-wing, more fundamentalist group. They believe in miracles, angels, raising the dead, and the entire Old Testament – all of which the Sadducees reject.

So Mark 12 continues with "Seeing that Jesus gave good answers to their questions, he asked Jesus, 'Which of the commands is most important?' Jesus answered, 'The most important command is this: Listen, people of Israel! [To which we should insert "people of America, your state, city, and church"] The Lord our God is the only Lord. Love the Lord your God with all your heart, all your soul, all your mind and all your strength.'"

Now, in answering the way He does, Jesus bundles some 3-4 aspects of a genuine, true, authentic, "Mountain Top" worship experience into one sentence. For instance, He says that true, real, genuine worship involves...

FOCUSING MY / OUR *ATTENTION ON* GOD

Look again at one part of what Jesus says in Mark's gospel: "The most important command [that is, it's priority one; it's non-optional, non-negotiable] is this: Love the Lord your God with all your...*mind.*" [Mark 12:29-30a, NCV]

In other words, our minds, brains, gray matter, our thought processes are to be fully engaged when it comes to loving and worshiping God. We don't just...

- "throw our minds into neutral",
- "zone out",
- engage in mental drift,
- wander, sleep, snore or text through worship;
- quit thinking and / or asking questions,
- become mechanical, or even think
- "It's all about me – my needs...what I want!"

In fact, as Bible teacher Warren Weirsbe puts it, *"We worship God because He is worthy and not because we...get something out of it. If we look upon worship only as a means of getting something from God, rather than giving something to God, then we make God our servant instead of our Lord and the elements of worship become a cheap formula for selfish gratification."* [Emphasis added.]

This is why The Message renders Paul's words to say that "Focusing on the self is the opposite of focusing on God. Anyone completely absorbed in self ignores God and ends up thinking more about self than God. That person ignores who God is and what he is doing." [Romans 8:7, TM]

And why does God want us to be so focused on Him?! Because He's so focused on *us*...and on *you!* In fact, one of the ongoing benefits of us *"focusing our attention* on *God"* is expressed by Isaiah where he says, "You will keep in perfect peace all who trust in you, whose thoughts are fixed on you!" [Isaiah 26:3, NLT]

However, along with focusing my [our] attention on God, Jesus also points out that real, genuine, authentic – true "Mountain Top" worship – involves us...

Again, as Jesus puts it: "The most important command is this… Love the Lord your God with all your [what?] *heart.*" [Or as The Message renders v. 30, "So love the Lord God with all your *passion and…energy.*" Mark 12:29-30, NCV, emphasis added.]

You see, just as Moses tells us that "He is a God who is passionate about his relationship with you" [Exodus 34:14, NLT], He wants us to be equally passionate – not passive – about Him! Whether in public or private, on Sunday or any day, on the mountain tops or down in the valleys of life – worship is always about God.

In fact, when you stop to think about it, the only real growth that occurs in our life usually isn't on a "mountain top"; it's down in the "valleys" of life. Because if you've ever actually climbed a mountain, once you pass the tree line at 11,000 feet, while it's often a great view, nothing grows on the summit.

Now, there are a number of biblical traits associated with worship and our expressing affection to God, and all of them involve activity, action, or us "doing" something. For instance:

- singing [Ephesians 5:19],
- dancing [Psalm 149:3],
- shouting [Psalm 27:6],
- playing instruments [Psalm 33:2-3],
- clapping [Psalm 47:1],
- bowing [Psalm 95:6]
- lifting hands [Psalm 63:4],
- commitment [Romans 12:1-2],
- praying [Psalm 95:6],
- giving [1 Corinthians 16:1-2],
- baptism [Romans 6:4],
- hearing the Word [John 17:17],
- meditating [Habakkuk 2:20], and
- Communion [or the Lord's Supper; 1 Corinthians 11:23-26].

You see, worship [as God intends and desires it to be] affects how we...

- live and work,
- play and give,
- sing and serve, and how
- we respond to Him – and each other – on Sunday and every other day of the week.

This is why God tells us, "I don't want your sacrifices – I want your love; I don't want your offerings – I want you to *know* me." [Hosea 6:6,

LB; emphasis added.] And again, the Hebrew word for *"know"* is *"yada".* It doesn't mean "to know intellectually"; it means *"to know intimately; to know experientially".*

In the midst of his message, a pastor friend of mine once said, *"Some of you are thinking, 'my problem is that I just don't love God enough...I just can't make myself love Him like I should."* [Then He adds] *That's not your problem. Your problem is that you don't realize how much He loves you! That's your problem. If you really knew how much God loves and cares about every detail of your life, you'd throw yourself at Him passionately!"*

So, if and when we're having or wanting to have a "mountain top" worship experience with God, Jesus is saying that it's seen when we're...

- focusing our *attention on* God,
- expressing our *affection to* God,

and then when I'm...

USING MY / OUT *ABILITIES FOR* GOD

Again, as Jesus tells us: "The most important command is this: Love the Lord your God with all your [what?] ...*strength.*'" [Mark 12:29-30,

NCV, emphasis added.] And what *"loving God with all (our)...strength"* means is loving Him with everything we've got! Our...

- talents and gifts,
- skills and time,
- work and recreation,
- abilities, disabilities, and even our liabilities.

You see, God uses us according to how He's "shaped" us. And using the word "SHAPE" as an acrostic, He uses us based on our...

- Spiritual gifts

As Paul puts it, "We have *different gifts*, according to the grace given us." [Romans 12:6a, NIV, emphasis added.] And Peter adds, "God *has given gifts to each of you* from his great variety of spiritual gifts. Manage them well so that God's generosity can flow through you." [1 Peter 4:10, NLT, emphasis added.]

Now there are a number of different studies and resources outlining the various gifts identified in Scripture; however, it's beyond the scope of this chapter to deal with them. One should, though, visit a local Christian bookstore to research this topic to see if he / she can discover that / those gift(s) God has entrusted to him / her.

And God uses us based, for the letter "H", on our...

- Heart

That is, what we do we have a heart for; what are we passionate about? Because as Moses expresses it, "Everyone who was willing and *whose heart moved him* came and brought an offering to the LORD." [Exodus 35:31, NIV, emphasis added.]

Some of us have a heart for people; others for computers, or sports, or mechanics, or...you get the idea.

One church I served as pastor had some members with a heart to serve the widows and single moms. A mechanic in our church opened his shop one Saturday each quarter so that the guys could change the oil, check the fluids and tire pressure, and even do some minor repair work on the gal's cars. The wives of the men served the women cookies and coffee while sitting with them as they watched their children. Not only were practical needs met, people's lives were changed.

Then, for the letter "A", our...

- Abilities

It may be some personal skill set, or an acquired trade or craft. Like the previous category, however, I have no skill when it comes to repairing cars. In fact, I like to tell mechanics that it's people like me that keep people like them in business.

And yet, as Moses puts it, "So...every skilled person to whom *the Lord has given skill and ability* to know how to carry out all the work of constructing the sanctuary are to do the work just as the Lord has commanded." [Exodus 36:1, NIV, emphasis added.]

Then, for the letter "P" of "Shape", our...

- Personality

Elijah was different than Elisha; Andrew wasn't anything like Peter, and; John the Baptist and Jesus were also different in how they approached ministry. In fact, consider how The Message renders Jesus' words in Matthew 11:16-19: "How can I account for this generation? The people have been like spoiled children whining to their parents, 'We wanted to skip rope and you were always too tired; we wanted to talk, but you were always too busy.' John came fasting and they called him crazy. I came feasting and they called me a lush, a friend of the riffraff. Opinion polls don't count for much, do they? The proof of the pudding is in the eating" [Or as the NLT puts it, "But wisdom is shown to be right by what results from it."]

Some people are ideal greeters; others are excellent counselors. Some are the quiet, more reserved types; some are like Peter: they walk into a room mouth first! The point being that God often uses us based on how we're "wired", our personality.

And for the letter "E" of "SHAPE", God uses our...

Experiences

And what sort of "experiences" do I mean? All of them. "The good, the bad, and the ugly"; the helpful and the hurtful; the ones we're glad we had; the ones we wish we'd never gone through. And yet, as Paul puts it, "[God] comes alongside us when we go through hard times and before you know it, he brings us alongside someone else who is going through hard times so that we can be there for that person just as God was there for us." [2 Corinthians 1:4, TM]

And we'll experience "Mountain Top" worship when or as we're engaged in the...

OFFERING OF OURSELVES TO GOD

Because the only way any of us can really *"love the Lord"* [Mark 12:30a] is if we've first established a personal relationship *with* the Lord. And how this happens is explained by Paul when he says that "If you confess with your mouth that Jesus is Lord and believe in your heart that God raised him from the dead, you will be saved." [Romans 10:9, NLT]

And then later he adds, "For anyone [no exceptions, no exclusions, no small print, no disclaimers – anyone!] who calls on the name of the Lord [Jesus] will be [what?] saved." [Romans 10:13, NLT]

You see, worshiping God – having some "Mountain Top" experience with God – isn't just for Sundays; it's for life. Consider how The Message renders Paul's words in Romans "Here's what I want you to do, God helping you:

Take your everyday, ordinary life – your sleeping, eating, going-to-work and walking-around life and place it before God as an offering. Embracing what God does for you is the best thing you can do for him." [Romans 12:1, TM]

So what, again, does our being on, or experiencing, a "Mountain Top" worship with our Lord actually mean and involve? That we'll be...

- focusing our *attention on* God,
- expressing our *affection to* God,
- using our *abilities for* God, and the
- offering of *ourselves to* God.

If you'd like to offer yourself to Christ – to know Him as your personal Lord and Savior – then there is a way, a prayer, to express that. Remember, though: becoming a real Christian is more than saying words. And yet, if you want Him to be in your heart and life, check out that prayer at the end of Chapter One.

Praying that prayer...and meaning it from your heart...will change your life, and your eternal destiny. And that way, you can know that you know you really *are* His child!

THE INCREDIBLE JOURNEY
Mapping the Christian Life
-Chapter 7-
Adversity: Overcoming Extreme Elements

Of all the words one might use to describe the Christian life, I doubt that the phrase "a walk in the park" would be some of them – at least from those of us who've been on this "journey" for any length of time.

And while it's true that the "view from a Mountain Top" [worship] can be both breathtaking and awe-inspiring, it's equally true [as noted earlier] that nothing actually grows on a mountain top: because above the tree line – which is 11,000 feet – it's barren, with no life and no vegetation. All of the greenery and growth is down on the lower slopes – in the deep valleys and open plains.

So at this point in our journey we're going to see how this is equally – if not especially – true with regard to our spiritual growth and development when we're faced with "extreme elements" on this Incredible Journey.

And what sort of "extreme elements" might we encounter in our physical world? Well there's everything from...

- blizzard-like conditions, to a
- blistering sun,
- torrential, monsoon rains,
- swollen rivers, to
- hurricanes,
- avalanches,
- snowstorms,
- firestorms,
- lightning storms,
- windstorms, and
- sandstorms.

Again, we're talking about "Overcoming Extreme Elements" on this Incredible Journey.

You see, the Christian life, this journey, isn't for the faint of heart or half-hearted. In fact, as Jesus tells us, "Here on earth you will have many trials and sorrows, but cheer up, for I have overcome the world." [John 16:33, LB] And the reason Jesus says this is because, since He lives in us, we too can overcome! Consider His words where He says: "But don't begin until you count the cost. For who would begin construction of a building without first getting estimates and then checking to see if there is enough money to pay the bills?... So no one can become my disciple

without giving up everything for me."
[Luke 14:28, 33, NLT]

And then, we even hear Paul say, "We all have to experience many hardships before we enter the kingdom of God." [Acts 14:22, Jerusalem Bible]

So, all this being true, then, what are some areas where we'll come face-to-face with some "extreme elements" in or on our spiritual journey? Well, there are actually two broad areas that are fairly common, the first of which involves our...

ENDURING UNEXPECTED "WHITEOUTS"

Now, in the physical or natural realm, people [like insurance companies and others] often refer to these events as "Acts of God". They're extremely dangerous, blizzard-like conditions that can spring up almost without notice or warning, sending us into shock or survival mode.

One of the worst on record occurred on January 12, 1888. It's called the "School Children's Blizzard." It was the "perfect storm", combining gale-force winds with rapidly falling temperatures [from 74 above-to-28 below zero], with 235 losing their lives.

Perhaps our longest-lasting "friends for the journey" are our dear friends Roger and Elaine Alford. We met in my second year of seminary. Although Roger and I are different in many ways, God has used him to give me "a word in due season" on more that one occasion. And my wife Terry counts Elaine as one of her dearest friends.

While in seminary, Roger became a pastor in western Kansas. And, on one occasion, when taking some vacation time to visit them, people asked me where we were going. I told them we were going to see some friends in Kansas. And they'd respond with, *"Nobody goes to Kansas. You're either going* through *Kansas or* over *Kansas to get to somewhere else. Nobody goes* to *Kansas!"*

Well, we did! We love Kansas, and we loved visiting our friends in Kansas. As I said, they're "friends for the journey."

In any case, they explained to me their experience with a whiteout. They'd been warned by parishioners what can happen when they occur, so they were also told how to prepare for one if it did. And did it!

One evening, while driving from Dodge City to their town Hanston [a forty mile trip] a snowstorm slammed down on them. And when it happened, they lost all points of reference. They said you couldn't see the headlights, hood of the car, horizon – they could barely see their hands in front of their faces.

They were told to carry survival gear in their car in order to ride it out. They were told they'd need a candle, shovel, sand, blankets, a can [you can figure that one out] and a newspaper. I did happen to ask why they needed the candle and newspaper. Was it to read the paper by candlelight in case you got bored? Maybe to stay warm? They said, *"Ah, no. Both were for warmth. You see, by putting the newspaper against your skin it will keep you warmer than the blanket!"*

Unfortunately, though advised to carry that gear, they'd failed to heed that advice. They were stranded in their car all night, struggling to stay warm. They survived; they also learned an invaluable life-lesson. Fortunately, a passing tractor-trailer rig spotted them at 10 the next morning.

Now, when it comes to our spiritual journey, the parallel is that whiteouts will also occur from time to time; they happen...

- with out warning,
- without advance notice, and
- without respect to the persons affected.

In other words, there are no exceptions, no exemptions, no exclusions, and no small print. All of us will – at some point or another, and some of us multiple times experience "whiteouts". Times when we feel frozen, isolated, immobilized, abandoned; when we lose all points of reference; when...

- God seems distant or absent;
- praying seems like a waste of time;
- Bible study is dry and lifeless; when
- church attendance seems like an exercise in futility; and even
- family or friends don't fully understand.

They may even make statements like, *"Why don't you just snap out of it?!"* Or *"Get over it!"* They haven't got a clue what you're going through. Now, Paul does give us some perspective on all this; sort of an advance warning, when he writes: "We can rejoice...when we run into problems and trials, for we know that they are good for us – they help us learn to endure. [We "learn" it; in other words, it doesn't come naturally; we aren't born with the ability to endure.] And endurance develops   strength of character in us, and character strengthens our confident expectation of salvation. And this expectation will not disappoint us. For we know how dearly God loves us, because he has given us the Holy Spirit to fill our hearts with his love." [Romans 5:3-5, NLT]

Or, as The Message paraphrases it, "There's more to come: We continue to shout our praise even when we're hemmed in with troubles, because we know how troubles can develop passionate patience in us and how that patience in turn forges the tempered steel of virtue, keeping us alert for whatever God will do next. In alert expectancy such as this, we're never left feeling shortchanged. Quite the contrary – we can't round up enough containers to hold everything God generously pours into our lives through the Holy Spirit!"

And yet, these spiritual whiteout, blizzard-like conditions where we seemingly lose our spiritual orientation most typically occur whenever we experience a...

- loss [through death, divorce, separation, abandonment – and we cry out God...*where are You, God?!*"];
- betrayal,
- rejection,
- personal failure, or
- [extended] unemployment,
- bankruptcy or financial reversals,
- sickness or illness,
- pain and suffering,
- being sexually violated,
- [extended] major disappointments; or
- senseless evil and / or
- mindless tragedies [i.e., 9/11, serial killers, terrorism, etc.].

It was St. John of the Cross – a Spanish mystic who lived in the mid-1500s – who once referred to what we're calling "whiteouts" as *"dark night(s) of the soul."*

And it's during times like these that we can shift into autopilot (spiritually speaking); we become numb to our environment; we pray but hear nothing; we confess every sin we can think of (or make up some others), but still we're the same. We fast, we wonder how long this "whiteout" might last. We wonder if it'll ever end. We stop thinking about God because we conclude that prayer (and He) don't matter anymore.

And, at the end of most days, we cry out in the night, "What's the matter with me?!"

And the answer? Nothing. *"Nothing?!"* you say?! Right. Nothing. Remember – we were told to expect this – that whiteouts would occur, and one has.

And a whiteout is precisely what Job – the one with the book named after him, [considered the oldest book of the Bible and a contemporary of Abraham] – experiences. In the midst of all his losses – his family, his financial portfolio, health, and judgment – he says: "If I go to the east, he [God] is not there; if I go to the west I do not find him. When he is at work in the north, I do not see him; when he turns to the south, I catch no glimpse of him." [Job 23:8-9, NIV]

Job's spiritually disoriented. Not hearing the "voice of God", or sensing the "nearness of God" he feels frozen, numb, out of control, trapped – like a dead man walking. And yet he goes on to say, "But he [God] knows the way that I take; when he has tested me, I will come forth as gold." [Job 23:10, NIV]

You see, this is why Paul tells us to "Endure hardship [NLT, "suffering"] with us like a good soldier of Christ Jesus." [2 Timothy 2:3, NIV] And why Hebrews 11:27 [NIV] reminds us that, regarding Moses, "By faith he left Egypt not fearing the king's anger; he persevered [NLT, "kept right on going"; KJV, "endured"] because he saw him who is invisible" [NAS, "unseen"– and don't confuse "unseen" with "unreal". While we obviously can't "see" air, we can certainly see its effects.]

And this is also why the writer of Hebrews asks: "Do you see what this means – all these pioneers who blazed the way, all these veterans cheering us on? It means we'd better get on with it. Strip down, start running and never quit! No extra spiritual fat, no parasitic sins. *Keep your eyes on Jesus*, who both began and finished this race we're in. Study how he did it. Because he never lost sight of where he was headed – that exhilarating finish in and with God – he could put up with anything along the way: cross, shame whatever. And now he's there, in the place of honor, right alongside God. When you find yourselves flagging in your faith, go over that story again, item by item, that long litany of hostility he plowed through. That will shoot adrenaline into your souls! In this all-out match against sin, others have suffered far worse than you, to say nothing of what Jesus went through – all that bloodshed!" [Hebrews 12:1-4, TM, emphasis added.]

And this is also why earlier, Hebrews records that "Then you will not become spiritually dull and indifferent. Instead, you will follow the example of those who are going to inherit God's promises because of their faith and patience." [NJB, "perseverance"] [Hebrews 6:12, NLT]

And it's also why we're told that "Let him who walks in the dark [the *"dark night of the soul"*] *who has no light,* trust in the name of the LORD and rely on his God."[Isaiah 50:10, NLT, emphasis added.]

Again, as The Message paraphrases Jesus' words, "I've told you all this so that trusting me, you will be unshakable and assured, deeply at peace. In this godless world you will continue to experience difficulties. But take heart! I've conquered the world." [John 16:33, TM]

So, when we think about it, author and theologian J.I. Packer is right when he says *"If we postpone our journey till the storm dies down, we may never get started at all."*

However, along with any "whiteouts", a second "extreme element" we'll often face on this Incredible Journey involves the challenge(s) of our...

OVERCOMING UNIMAGINABLE "FIRESTORMS"

Nearly every summer there are a number of firestorms out west that scorch literally hundreds to thousands of acres – with people losing their houses, businesses, possessions, and some even losing their lives. And nearly all of them are set off by natural causes– lightning; sometimes by a careless camper, or they're intentionally started.

In any case, firestorms are another type of "extreme element" that we'll encounter or experience as Christ-followers. As Peter puts it, "I beg you not to be unduly alarmed at the fiery ordeals which come to test your faith, as though this were some abnormal experience." [1 Peter 4:12, Modern English]

And a "fiery ordeal" or "firestorm" is typically anything that doesn't qualify as a white-out; we refer to them as...

- "trials and tribulations",
- difficulties,
- stressors,
- financial pressures,
- people problems,
- marital conflicts,
- legal hassles,
- temptations, and
- "tough times".

And it isn't at all uncommon for us to think – or entertain thoughts – about "bailing out" on this so-called Incredible Journey when whatever "firestorm" we encounter or are going through isn't extinguished very quickly. We think or say, "Hey, I didn't sign up for this! I'm outta here! I'm headin' back to base camp!"

Consider our friend Sharon Wilson. A believer for barely a year she related to me that she'd undergone a month-long mental, emotional, and spiritual siege where she felt totally disoriented. She couldn't understand why she was in such a funk.

She was snapping at her co-workers, on the outs with her family, and couldn't understand at all why she was having such a major challenge to "living the Christian life." She thought all she needed to do was accept Christ and her life would be a breeze. I and others did warn her about not thinking like that. And her most special friend, Pam Reynolds, was (and still is) her mentor, coaching her through Bible studies and giving her invaluable personal and godly counsel.

However, this particular truth wasn't one Sharon grasped, at least not initially during her first year as a new believer. Alas, some "journey lessons" can only be learned by experience. She struggled; she wanted to bail on what she called "this whole Christian-life thingy!"

But then a couple of friends at her church – Bob and Glenice Anthony – gave her a call. Bob recommended some books for her to read. And though Sharon admitted she isn't much of a reader, she found what she needed to know in those books. What she learned helped pull her back from the "edge of the cliff" and bailing out on the Christian life.

She learned that all she was going through was "normal" in the Christian life. And that God was using all of these experiences to "grow her up" in her walk with Him. As she put it to me, "she broke through!" And then she was able to put words to her experiences, realizing that God was in all of what she was going through to draw her closer to Him, and take her deeper in Him.

And isn't this what Jesus tells us to expect?

As C.S. Lewis put it, *"[This] is why [Jesus] warned people to 'count the cost' [cf., Luke 14:28] before becoming Christians. 'Make no mistake,' [Lewis has Jesus saying] 'if you let me, I will make you perfect. The moment you put yourself in My hands, that is what you are in for. Nothing less, or other, than that. You have free will, and if you choose, you can push Me away. But if you do not push Me away, understand that I am going to see this job through. Whatever suffering it may cost you in your earthly life, whatever it costs Me, I will never rest, nor let you rest until you are literally perfect – until my Father can say without reservation that He is well pleased with you, as He said He was well pleased with me. This I can do and will do. But I will not do anything less."*

Well, knowing that we'll experience "whiteouts" and "firestorms" is one thing; overcoming them is another.

So, how do we survive, overcome, or even thrive in spite of them? As a general rule of thumb, enduring and / or overcoming spiritual whiteouts and firestorms basically requires two elements. The first involves us having access to the right...

Information

In other words, we need to know both *what to expect* and *how to respond* to these experiences. In many cases, we learn what we need to know from outside sources – like the Bible, books, CDs, the Internet, people, counselors, seminars, workshops, conferences, etc.

However, a lot of our "learning" comes from experience – from the "School of Hard Knocks" where our "school colors" are black and blue (and sometimes red). As even Aldous Huxley – who isn't one you typically quote for spiritual advice – once observed, *"Experience is not what [actually] happens to you. It is what you do with what happens to you."* Which is why Isaiah tells us that "It was for my own good that I had such hard times." [Isaiah 38:17, CEV]

And why is that? Because "whiteouts" and "firestorms" have a way of. . .

- purifying our motives [Psalm 139:23-24; Psalm 51:1-10];
- testing and refining our faith[1 Peter 1:6-7; Deuteronomy 8:2ff];
- maturing us [James 1:2-4; Romans 5:3-5], and;
- giving us a "message" to share with others [2 Corinthians 1:3-4].

And in truth, a "message" that only comes from our heads will only reach a head, but a "message" that comes from our life will impact a life. Actually, I even think M. Scott Peck, in his book *The Road Less Traveled*, also gives us some rather insightful "insider information" regarding "life's journey" when he says, *"Life is difficult. This is a great truth, one of the greatest truths. It is a great truth because once we truly see this truth, we transcend it. Once we truly understand and accept it then life is no longer difficult. Because once it is accepted, the fact that life is difficult no longer matters."*
Of course, that being said, we still need to have a working knowledge of information contained in our "Guide Book" [the Bible], because, as David tells us, "By them is your servant warned and in keeping of them there is great reward." [Psalm 19:11, NIV] And the "them" he's referring to are the statutes, precepts, commands, warnings,

instructions, guide-lines, promises, principles and truths of God's Word.

And yet, information in and of or by itself is useless, unless it's coupled with...

Application

Again, as Jesus tells us, "If you know these things, happy are you if you [what? *Know* them? *Read* them? *Quote* them? *Memorize* 'em? Have a *Bible study* about them? No.] Do them." [John 13:17, KJV, emphasis mine.]

So, as The Message paraphrases James as saying in chapter 1:22 of his book, "Don't fool yourself into thinking that you are a listener when you are anything but, letting the Word go in one ear and out the other. Act on what you hear!" You see, just as we learn how to...

- drive by driving,
- swim by swimming,
- text by texting, and
- hunt by hunting...
- we also learn to...
- love by loving,
- forgive by forgiving,
- endure by enduring,

- persevere by persevering,
- trust by trusting, and
- obey by obeying.

So, when it comes to us surviving and even thriving in the midst of our whiteouts or fire-storms, as Paul tells us, "Keep putting into practice [*application*] all you learned [*information*] and the God of peace will be with you." [Philippians 4:9, NLT]

Knowing these twin truths – and applying them – will definitely improve our odds of survival on this Incredible Journey!

THE INCREDIBLE JOURNEY
Mapping the Christian Life
-Chapter 8-
Temptations: Enemies of the Wild

What comes to mind when you think of a predatory animal...apart from man, that is? Well, after checking the Animal Planet web site, I found two primary categories of predators: cats and snakes [or reptiles].

Now, regarding the cat family, those listed as predators include:

- lions and tigers,
- leopards,
- panthers,
- lynx,
- bobcats,
- jaguars, and
- cheetahs.

However, in many respects, the snake family comes across as far more deadly.

For instance, the Reticulated Python can grow up to 30 feet, and weighs-in at up to 240 pounds, killing its prey by constriction. And yet, not to be outdone, the Anaconda – though only growing to

29 feet – weighs-in at 500 pounds, and it can swallow a jaguar. [another predator, not the car. Sorry, I couldn't resist.]

Then there's the Krait Snake with venom that's 16 times stronger than a cobra's. And the Black (and Green) Mamba strikes fear to an African at the mere mention of its name. It can grow up to 14 feet, hit a speed of 15 mph, and possesses venom that kills within minutes.

I'm sure we'd all agree that these would qualify as enemies of the wild.

Well, as you might suspect, there's a striking parallel between these enemies of the wild and what we'll encounter in the spiritual realm on this Incredible Journey known as the Christian life. And this is especially true with regard to temptations from "The Snake". For as Moses tells us, "Now the serpent was the shrewdest of all the creatures the Lord God had made. 'Really?' he asked the woman. 'Did God really say you must not eat any of the fruit in the garden?'" [Genesis 3:1, NLT]

The fact is, our "Guide Book" [the Bible in chapter 3] is quite explicit when it comes to informing hiker wanna-be's what sort of spiritual "enemies of the wild" we're up against, and how these "enemies", like certain cats and snakes, don't "play games", they "play for keeps".

And yet, Paul also tells us that "No test or temptation that comes your way is beyond the course of what others have had to face. All you need to remember is that God will never let you down; he'll never let you be pushed past your limit; he'll always be there to help you come through it." [1 Corinthians 10:13, TM]

And Peter tells us that "The Lord knows how to deliver the godly out of temptations..." [2 Peter 2:9a, NKJV] And even James reminds us to "Humble yourselves before God. Resist the Devil and he will flee from you." [James 4:7, NLT]

However, what are some temptations or "enemies of the wild" we'll encounter? Where will they come from; from what direction? Well, one of our enemies involves us...

RESISTING A SEDUCTIVE "PREDATORY CULTURE"

Now, I realize, of course, that the word "culture" may be misleading, as the word itself can mean different things to different people. For many people, the word "culture" is neither good nor bad, it just is. Some may associate or think of culture in the classical sense, like one dictionary that defines it as the *"development, improvement, or refinement of the intellect, emotions, interests, manners and taste."*

And yet, this isn't the only definition of culture. It's also how we think, live and behave as a people. Our morality; our innate sense of right and wrong; reality; the way we see ourselves and others.

So, with those understandings in mind, what sort of mind set or sense of right and wrong are we being exposed to, inundated by, and saturated with on a daily, nearly moment-by-moment basis from every possible angle, imaginable venue, and social outlet? Well, consider what Pulitzer Prize-winning columnist Ellen Goodman says as she gives her assessment of the "predatory nature" of our culture in a powerful editorial where she writes: *"At some point between Lamaze and PTA, it becomes clear that one of your main jobs as a parent is to counter the culture. What the media deliver to children by the masses, you are expected to rebut one at a time...Mothers and fathers are expected to screen virtually every aspect of their children's lives. To check the ratings on movies, to read the labels on CDs, to find out if there's MTV in the house next door. All the while keeping touch with school and in their free time earning a living. It isn't that they can't say no. It's that there's so much more to say no to. Without wallowing in false nostalgia there has been a fundamental shift. American's once expected parents to raise their children in accordance with the dominant cultural messages. Today they are expected to raise their children in opposition."*

And in Galatians 5:17-21 we find both a graphic and accurate New Testament assessment regarding our "predatory culture" as anything else we could point to around us. As The Message paraphrases it, "It is obvious what kind of life develops out of trying to get your own way all the time: repetitive, loveless, cheap sex; a stinking accumulation of mental and emotional garbage; frenzied and joyless grabs for happiness; cut-throat competition; all-consuming-yet-never-satisfied wants; a brutal temper; an impotence to love and be loved; divided homes and divided lives; small-minded and lopsided pursuits; the vicious habit of depersonalizing everyone into a rival; uncontrolled and uncontrollable addictions; ugly parodies of community. I could go on."

So, one "Enemy of the Wild" or source of temptation, then, is our seductive "predatory culture". Small wonder why John warns us by saying: "Don't love the world's ways. Don't love the world's goods. The 'love of the world' [like a Reticulated Python] squeezes out love for the Father. Practically everything that goes on in the world – wanting your own way, wanting everything for yourself, wanting to appear important – has nothing to do with the Father. It just isolates you from him. The world and all its wanting, wanting, wanting is on the way out – but whoever does what God wants is set for eternity." [1 John 2:15-17, TM]

And then, as Paul adds, "Don't copy the behavior and customs of this world, but let God transform you into a new person by changing the way you think. Then you will know what God wants you to do and you will know how good and pleasing and perfect his will really is." [Romans 12:1-2, NLT]

And yet, along with Resisting a Seductive "Predatory Culture", another "Enemy of the Wild" requires that we secondly begin...

"STANDING UP" AGAINST DEMONIC INFLUENCE

Now, this is can be a bit more challenging because these forces or influences are often "off the grid"; they're at work "behind the scenes" and / or are "under the radar".

And yet, as Paul tells us, often "we are not fighting against people made of flesh and blood, but against persons without bodies - the evil rulers of the unseen world, those mighty satanic beings and great evil princes of darkness who rule this world and against huge numbers of wicked spirits in the spirit world." [Ephesians 6:12, LB] And then he adds, "So use every piece of God's armor to resist the enemy whenever he attacks and when it is all over, you will still be standing up." [Ephesians 6:13, LB]

We'll come back to this verse in just a bit.

I realize that not everyone believes in demonic influences or a personal devil; however, according to a Gallup Poll, 40% of American's claim to have seen, heard or felt the presence of a ghost. And though some try to "cross over" and make contact with the dead, God specifically condemns any effort on our part to do so [Leviticus 19:31; 20:6, 27; Deuteronomy 18:11-12; 1 Samuel 28:7].

You see, regardless and whether it is through or by means of a...

- Channeler,
- séance,
- Ouija boards,
- palm readers,
- tarot cards, or
- the occult

God explicitly says, "NO! You don't want to go there!" And why do you suppose God forbids it? Is it to keep "something really good" *from* us? Hardly. It's to keep "something very bad" from happening *to* us. That is, exposing ourselves to what the Bible calls a "familiar spirit", which is a demon. If you open yourself (or your spirit) up to that influence, you are setting yourself up for both demonic oppression and, if taken further, demonic possession.

And Jesus, who refers to Satan twenty-five times as being an actual person or entity – not just a "force" or the "dark side"; someone who'd win a look-alike contest with *Star Wars* Sith Lord Darth Maul along with others in the New Testament, are explicit about demonic / satanic realities, with Satan [the Devil] being our primary *"Enemy of the Wild!"*

Now, he goes by a number of aliases: he's called or referred to as the...

- Destroyer,
- Accuser,
- Murderer,
- Evil One,
- Liar,
- Adversary,
- Deceiver,
- Great Dragon,
- Father of lies,
- Tempter, the
- "cherub that covers", the
- "god of this age", the
- Wicked One, and an
- "Angel of light".

And he's also known by two other names or titles, both of which underscores his predatory nature – like the two classes of predators we noted at the outset of this chapter. As Peter warns us, "Be careful – watch out for attacks from Satan, your great enemy. He prowls around like a [predator; a] hungry, roaring *lion*, looking for some victim to tear apart." [1 Peter 5:8, LB, emphasis added.] And then John tells us that he's referred to as "the ancient *serpent* called the devil, or Satan, the one deceiving the whole world." [Revelation 12:9, LB, emphasis added.]

Evil is not static; it's active, eternal, seemingly omnipresent, and highly contagious. Never doubt for a moment that while God loves us and has a wonderful plan for our lives, Satan hates us and has a horrible plan for our lives.

So, on this Incredible Journey, then, there are some very real, very deadly "Enemies of the Wild".

And yet, along with a "Predatory Culture" and "Demonic Influences", there's a third "Enemy of the Wild" we'll have to confront, overcome and deal with, and that involves...

"DYING" TO OUR "FLESHLY NATURE"

Or our "flesh" [also called our "old nature"]; what the Bible refers to as our "old man" or our carnal [our "B.C." = "before Christ"] human nature. When we're acting out of our "B.C" condition, that's when we [again] tend to think we're a combination of Dr. Jekyll and Mr. Hyde. And while it's one thing to believe you're being chased by the devil, it's an entirely different matter to think you've become – or are becoming – a devil. Consider how Paul puts it:

"I don't understand myself at all, for I really want to do what is right, but I can't. I do what I don't want to – what I hate. I know perfectly well that what I am doing is wrong and my bad conscience proves that I agree with these laws I am breaking. But I can't help myself....It is sin inside me that is stronger than I am that make me do these evil things. I know I am rotten through and through so far as my old sinful [i.e., "fleshly", human, carnal] nature is concerned. No matter which way I turn I can't make myself do right. I want to but I can't. When I want to do good, I don't and when I try not to do wrong, I do it anyway." [Romans 7:15-19, LB]

Can any of us relate to this? I know I can. Then in the very next chapter he adds, "My dear friends, we must not live to satisfy our desires. If you do, you will die. But you will live, if by the help of God's Spirit you say 'No' to your desires." [Romans 8:12-13, CEV]

Or, as a couple of other translations render his words in v. 13 [TEV]: "For if you live according to your human [GW, "corrupt"] nature, you are going to die; but if by the Spirit [GW, "if you use your spiritual nature to put to death the evil activities of the body"] [NCV, "the wrong things you do with your body"; NJB, "the habits originating in the body"] you will live."

And then The Message paraphrases Paul saying in Colossians 3:5, "And that means killing off everything connected with that way of death: sexual promiscuity, impurity, lust, doing whatever you feel like whenever you feel like it and grabbing whatever attracts your fancy. That's a life shaped by things and feelings instead of by God."

Small wonder why the cartoon character Pogo once said, *"We have met the enemy and they is us!"*

Which is why Jesus says, "If anyone chooses to be my disciple [that is, if we sign up and begin this Incredible Journey] he must say 'No' to self, put the cross on his shoulders daily and continue to follow me." [Luke 9:23, Williams] Not follow some rules, rituals and religious regulations religion about God; rather, it's all about having a living, on-going, day-to-day relationship with God.

Well, as any hunter would say, if you're "out in

the wild", you'd better have the right weapon for whatever "enemy of the wild" you face. And in a similar sense, Paul tells us that: "The truth is that, although we lead normal human lives the battle we are fighting is on the spiritual level. The very weapons we use are not human but powerful in God's warfare for the destruction of the enemy's strongholds." [2 Corinthians 10:3-4, Modern English]

And then, The Message renders v. 5 as saying, "We use our powerful God-tools for smashing warped philosophies, tearing down barriers erected against the truth of God, fitting every loose thought and emotion and impulse into the structure of life shaped by Christ."

So, with all this in view, let's use the word "weapons" as an acrostic or acronym to identify what we need to overcome The Tempter, temptations or our "Enemies of the Wild". It requires [for the letter "W" of "weapons"] our wearing the right...

Wardrobe

Here's how Paul puts it: "Put on all of God's armor so that you will be able to stand firm against all strategies and tricks of the Devil. For we are not fighting against people made of flesh and blood, but against the evil rulers and authorities of the unseen world, against those mighty powers of darkness who rule this world, and against wicked spirits in the heavenly realms. Use every piece of God's armor to resist the enemy in the time of evil, so that after the battle you will still be standing firm. Stand your ground, putting on the sturdy belt of truth and the body armor of God's righteousness. For shoes, put on the peace that comes from the Good News, so that you will be fully prepared. In every battle you will need faith as your shield to stop the fiery arrows aimed at you by Satan. Put on salvation as your helmet, and take the sword of the Spirit, which is the word of God." [Ephesians 6:11-17, NLT]

Years ago, when my wife was a teenager, she said it use to wear her out "putting on" all that armor every day! Then one happy day she heard her pastor quote Romans 14:13a of "put (ting) on the Lord Jesus" and then add, "If you 'put on' Jesus, you're putting on all that armor, because He is your salvation, righteousness, truth, gospel and Word!" Ah, sweet release!

You see, by choosing to submit to Jesus' Lordship and rule in her life, she was "putting on the Lord

Jesus". So, as Paul puts, "For all of you who were baptized into Christ have clothed yourselves with Christ." [Galatians 3:27, NIV]

And for the letter "E", we need an...

Exit Strategy

And regarding this truth Paul tells us to "Run away from sexual sin! [KJV, "flee fornication"; and here the Greek word for "fornication" is "*porneia*", from which we get our English word pornography.] No other sin so clearly affects the body as this one does. For sexual immorality is a sin against your own body." [1 Corinthians 6:18, NLT]

And then in one of his pastoral letters Paul adds, "Run from anything that gives you the evil thoughts that young men often have, but stay close to anything that makes you want to do right. Have faith and love, and enjoy the companionship of those who love the Lord and have pure hearts." [2 Timothy 2:22, LB]

By the way, a great example of this strategy is found in the Old Testament life of Joseph in Genesis 39. Sold into slavery by his brothers, Joseph ends up in Egypt, and bought by a man named Potiphar. Although the KJV only says that Potiphar was "an officer of Pharaoh, captain of the guard" [Genesis 39:1b], he was actually the chief executioner. He was in charge of eliminating Pharaoh's enemies.

However, Joseph proves himself to be an invaluable slave. As we're told: "The Lord was with Joseph and blessed him greatly as he served in the home of his Egyptian master. Potiphar noticed this and realized that the Lord was with Joseph, giving him success in everything he did. So Joseph naturally became quite a favorite with him. Potiphar soon put Joseph in charge of his entire household and entrusted him with all his business dealings." [Genesis 39:2-4]

Potiphar has a wife; however, though no name is given, she's on the prowl. And as we can read, "About this time, Potiphar's wife began to desire [Joseph] and invited him to sleep with her." [Genesis 39:7, NLT] Why? Because as the previous verse relates, "Joseph was a very handsome and well-built young man." [Genesis 39:6c, NLT]

So how does Joseph respond? Does he take a "When in Rome – or Egypt – do as the Romans do?"

Nope.

As we can read: "But Joseph refused. 'Look,' he told her, 'my master trusts me with everything in his entire household. No one here has more authority than I do! He has held back nothing from me except you, because you are his wife. How could I ever do such a wicked thing? It would be a great sin against God." [Genesis 39:8-9, NLT]

Well, "Mrs. Potiphar" is not so easily dissuaded. And as we're told, "She kept putting pressure on him day after day, but he refused to sleep with her, and he kept out of her way as much as possible." [Genesis 39:10, NLT] Finally, she corners him. With no one seemingly around, "She...grabbed him by his shirt, demanding, 'Sleep with me!'" [Genesis 39:12a]

And how does young Joseph respond? He executes his "exit strategy" by showing temptation his heels, for we read that "Joseph tore himself away, but as he did, his shirt came off. She was left holding it as he ran from the house." [Genesis 39:12b, NLT] Or as the KJV puts it so bluntly, "he...got him out."

Yes, there's more to the story. "Mrs. P" frames

him on a morals charge ["Hell hath no fury..."] her hubby throws him into a prison for political prisoners. [Actually, if Potiphar really believed her story, he would have killed Joseph. He knows his wife; he knows Joseph. But he has to "save face"...so Joseph languishes in an even deeper cell for an additional two years. Cf. Genesis 40:1-41:1].

And yet God is still at work in Joseph's life, ruling above and through his circumstances. He "takes up his case", using all that he goes through to prepare him for his future "ministry" as Prime Minister of Egypt.

But we have to ask: would that be the way the story would have ended for Joseph had he caved, had he spiritually cratered and catered to the "Mrs."?

We are left to wonder. I suspect not.

Sometimes the best offense is a good defense.

And yet, for the letter "A" we need...

Accountability

This is when we have a partner whom we can

call to pray for us, and we for him or her. Herein lies one of the benefits that the writer of Hebrews speaks of when he writes, "And let us not neglect our meeting together, as some people do, but encourage and warn each other, especially now that the day of his coming back again is drawing near." [Hebrews 10:25, NLT]

And it's initially identified by Luke in Acts where he records that "...those who believed Peter were baptized about 3,000 all! They joined with the other believers in regular attendance at the apostles' teaching sessions and at the Communion services and prayer meetings." [Acts 2:41-42, LB]

That setting provided the environment for accountability!

And, for the letter "P", we need to be engaged in honest, heart-searching...

Prayer

Or, as Paul puts it, "Always keep on praying." [KJV, "Pray without ceasing." 1 Thessalonians 5:17, LB] And then, in another letter Paul adds, "Pray at all times and on every occasion in the power of the Holy Spirit. Stay alert and be persistent in your prayers for all Christians everywhere." [Ephesians 6:18, NLT] And as the Message renders Jesus' words in Matthew 6:6-8: "Here's what I want you to do: Find a quiet, secluded place so you won't be tempted to role-play before God. Just be there as simply and honestly as you can manage. The focus will shift from you to God, and you will begin to sense his grace. The world is full of so-called prayer warriors who are prayer-ignorant. They're full of formulas and programs and advice, peddling techniques for getting what you want from God. Don't fall for that nonsense. This is your Father you are dealing with, and he knows better than you what you need."

Indeed!

You see, this kind of praying isn't some little "no I lay me down to sleep" / "God is great, God is good" kind of praying. This is an intense, concentrated, focused, practical and targeted kind of praying.

And for the letter "O" of our "weapons" we need to give whole-hearted...

Obedience

As Jesus puts it, "You know these things – now do them! That is the path of blessing." [John 13:17, NLT] And then later He challenges us by asking, "So why do you call me 'Lord' when you won't obey me?" [John 6:46, LB]

It's not what we *know* that will change our lives; it's what we *do* with what we know that makes the difference. And let's have the letter "N" represent or stand for...

No Compromise

Or no defection. Consider how the writer of Hebrews puts it: "Since we have such a huge crowd of men of faith watching us from the grandstands, let us strip off anything that slows us down or holds us back and especially those sins that wrap themselves so tightly around our feet and trip us up and let us run with patience the particular race that God has set before us." [Hebrews 12:1, LB]

Hold your ground; don't make any "deals" with the devil; As Paul puts it, "Therefore put on the full armor of God, so that when the day of evil comes, you may be able to *stand your ground,* and after you have done everything, *to stand.*" [Ephesians 6:13, NIV, emphasis added.]

And the "S" of our "weapons" identifies our need to be...

Spirit-filled

Because living the Christian life isn't difficult; it's not even hard...it's impossible. Only Jesus ever lived the "Christian life". And if we're to do it we have to be yielded to the controlling presence and power of the Holy Spirit!

As Paul puts it, "Don't drink too much wine, for many evils lie along that path; be filled instead with the Holy Spirit and controlled by him." [Ephesians 5:18, NLT] Then, in Romans Paul adds, "But clothe yourselves with [NKJV, "put on"] the Lord Jesus Christ and forget about satisfying your sinful self." [Romans 13:14, NCV]

What God's promising us is that by our having the right "weapons", and using them at the right time, He'll enable us to emerge as winners whenever we encounter any "Enemy of the Wild"!

THE INCREDIBLE JOURNEY
Mapping The Christian Life
-Chapter 9-
Hypocrisy: Avoiding Hazardous Hikers

Sometimes Christians can act so, well, "un-Christian".

Whether it's by our attitudes, behavior, reactions, how we talk or treat others, it isn't too hard to see why some people are "put off" by our so-called "Christianity" – which looks and feels a lot more like "churchianity". Perhaps this is why we so often hear non-Christians and / or unchurched people accusing Christians of being phony, artificial, or even hypocrites, one trait that is universally despised and detested by all people, be they Christian, unchurched, or non-Christian.

The word itself means to be "two-faced", to "play a role"; an actor...and that's what I mean when I'm talking about "hazardous hikers". It's when those who profess to be Christian act as if they're any but. Allow me to add, though, that a hypocrite isn't someone who may occasionally blow it as a Christian. The hypocrite term often gets thrown into someone's face who may "drop the ball" spiritually. Or else they'll hear, *"And you call yourself a Christian!"*

Actually, a hypocrite [biblically-speaking] is someone who intentionally projects one image on the outside while in reality he or she is a completely different person on the inside.

In fact, it's these sorts of "hazardous hikers" that caused Philip Yancey to relate the story of a Chicago prostitute unable to buy food for her two-year-old daughter. When her friend asked if she had ever thought of going to a church for help, she cried, *"Church! Why would I ever go there? I was already feeling terrible about myself. They'd just make me feel worse!"*

Great.

Why is this true? I mean, how does it happen that so many "hikers" on this Incredible Journey are "kicked out of camp", "knocked off the trail" or even "thrown off the mountain"? Well, people in general – and especially new "hikers" or Christians – can become disillusioned with the Christian life and church for a lot of understandable reasons, like:

- conflict and hurt
[i.e., like when church business meetings

become "battle grounds and war zones"];
- neglect;
- pettiness [get feelings hurt or feeling slighted];
- judgmentalism [a "better-than-you" or "holier-than-thou" attitude]
- prejudice;
- scandal or weird teachings

[The daily news features them all: Jim Bakker, Rev. Moon, Jim Jones, and Applewhite's "Heaven's Gate" (Halley's Comet), David Koresh at Waco, et al.]

I remember a story of a young man who'd been exploited by religious leaders and feeling frustrated and disillusioned, he fled to Mexico and began immersing himself in drugs. Well, he ended up running into some former drug dealers who'd recently become Christians. They shared Christ with him and prayed for him. So, he went home with a renewed passion for Christ; however, after entering a bookstore he asked the manager, *"Do you have any books by dead Christians? I don't trust anybody living!"*

Can you relate? I know I can.

And it's because hypocrisy is so hazardous, so

toxic to another's spiritual life and progress that Peter tells us to "Get rid of all malicious behavior and deceit. Don't just pretend to be good! Be done with hypocrisy and jealousy and backstabbing." [1 Peter 2:1, NLT]

In fact, Jesus has a few choice words for some religious-type people when He says: "How terrible it will be for you teachers of religious law and you Pharisees. *Hypocrites*! For you won't let others enter the Kingdom of Heaven, and you won't go in yourselves....How terrible it will be for you teachers of religious law and you Pharisees. *Hypocrites*! For you are careful to tithe even the tiniest part of your income, but you ignore the important things of the law - justice, mercy, and faith. You should tithe, yes, but you should not leave undone the more important things...How terrible it will be for you teachers of religious law and you Pharisees. *Hypocrites*! You are so careful to clean the outside of the cup and the dish, but inside you are filthy – full of greed and self-indulgence...How terrible it will be for you teachers of religious law and you Pharisees. *Hypocrites*! You are *like* whitewashed tombs – beautiful on the outside but filled on the inside with dead people's bones and all sorts of impurity...How terrible it will be for you teachers of religious law and you Pharisees. *Hypocrites*!

For you build tombs for the prophets your ancestors killed and decorate the graves of the godly people your ancestors destroyed." [Matthew 23:13, 23, 25, 25, 29, NLT, emphasis added.]

As The Message paraphrases Jesus' words to an earlier audience in Matthew 23:3, "You won't go wrong in following their [the Pharisees] teachings on Moses [the Torah or first five books of the Old Testament]. But be careful about following *them*. They talk a good line, but they don't live it. They don't take it into their hearts and live it out in their behavior. It's all spit-and-polish veneer." [Emphasis added.]

Well, then, as it relates to the Christian life – to those on this Incredible Journey – what might help some "hikers" is for us to have a couple "reality checks" with regard to certain "hazardous hikers" on this Journey. For instance, let's consider...

REALITY CHECK #1:
All "Christ-followers" *are not following Christ!*

You see, the truth is, some so-called Christians are actually...

- manipulators and / or control-freaks

We find one example of this where the apostle John is paraphrased as saying, "Diotrephes, who loves being in charge, denigrates my counsel. If I come, you can be sure I'll hold him to account. for spreading vicious rumors about us. As if that weren't bad enough, he not only refuses hospitality to traveling Christians but tries to stop others from welcoming them. Worse yet, instead of inviting them in, he throws them out." [3 John 1:9-10, TM]

Then there are those who are...

- self-serving and / or self-centered

Now Jesus warns us about these sorts of people when He says: "Everything they do is done for show....They pretend to be holy, with long, public prayers... while...evicting widows from their homes." [Matthew 23:4, 14, LB]

And sometimes a "hiker" can get "kicked off the trail" or "off the mountain" due to a...

- betrayer (or betrayal) and / or disloyalty

This seems to be what an earlier "hiker" [David] experienced when he records that: "It was not an enemy who taunted me - then I could have borne it; I could have hidden and escaped. But it was you, a man like myself, my companion and my friend. What fellowship we had, what wonderful discussions as we walked together to the Temple of the Lord [i.e., church] on holy days." [Psalm 55:12-14, LB]

Or we encounter "hikers" who (again) are...

- judgmental

Now, to be sure, Jesus tells us: "Do not judge, or you too will be judged....Why do you look at the speck of sawdust in your brother's eye and pay no attention to the plank [i.e., the 2x4] in your own eye? You *hypocrite*. First take the plank out of your own eye, and then you will see clearly to remove the speck from your brother's eye." [Matthew 7:1, 3, 5, NIV, emphasis added.]

Have you ever been on the "receiving end" of this? I know I have! For the clothes I wear, the hairstyle I have, the car I drive...and on it goes.

And some "hikers" are just flat out...

- legalistic

You know, where they're driven by the "do's and don'ts" of religion; it's as if they're always talking about keeping some rule, ritual, or regulation. "The Constitution and By-laws says this!" "The Church Covenant says that!" "The book of Leviticus says…" You get the point.

Sometimes we can be guilty of having a higher standard than God.

To be sure, we need and must care about what God says in His Word; however, people like this don't use it as a scalpel to heal, they use it as a sledgehammer to kill. These are the kind of "hikers" Jesus refers to when He talks of those "[who] strain out a gnat and swallow a camel." [Matthew 23:24, NIV] And again, Mark records where Jesus replied: "You bunch of *hypocrites*! Isaiah the prophet described you very well when he said, "These people speak very prettily about the Lord but they have no love for him at all. Their worship is a farce, for they claim that God commands the people to obey their petty rules." How right Isaiah was! For you ignore God's specific orders and substitute your own traditions. You are simply rejecting God's laws and trampling them under your feet for the sake of tradition." [Mark 7:6-9, LB, emphasis added.]

Again, I love how author and Pastor Chuck Swindoll puts it: *"Being free, enjoying your liberty and allowing others the same enjoyment is hard to do if you're insecure. It is especially hard to do if you were raised by legalistic parents and led by legalistic pastors with an over-sensitive conscience toward pleasing everyone. Those kinds of parents and pastors can be ultra-controlling, manipulative, and judgmental. Frequently they use the Bible as a hammer to pound folks into submission rather than as a guide to lead others to grace. Sometimes it takes years for people who have been under a legalistic cloud to finally have the courage to walk freely in the grace of God."*

And we also need to be on the look-out for "hikers" who wittingly or unwittingly, knowingly or unknowingly give us "bad instructions" or...

- wrong teaching

Or what I'd otherwise call warped, twisted teaching, bad advice, or "ungodly (unbiblical or not biblically balanced) counsel". As Matthew records it: "'Watch out!' Jesus warned them. 'Beware of the yeast of the Pharisees and Sadducees.' They [the apostles] decided he was saying this because they hadn't brought any bread. Then at last they understood that he wasn't speaking about yeast or bread but about the *false teaching* of the Pharisees and Sadducees." [Matthew 16:6-7, NLT, emphasis added.]

And if the truth be told, some so-called Christians or "hikers" are actually just plain...

- lost

Because as Jesus puts it, "Yes, woe upon you *hypocrites*. For you go to all lengths to make one convert, and then turn him into twice the son of hell you are yourselves." [Matthew 23:15, LB, emphasis added.]

Now, if or when we encounter a "hazardous hiker", and are negatively affected (or "infected"!) by him or her, we'll often go through a series of stages of grief:

STAGE 1: shock and / or surprise

This is when we or others say things like, *"Man, I never thought he / she'd could do something like that!"* Well, if we don't process this and get it resolved at this stage, then we hit...

STAGE 2: disappointment

This is where we begin saying things like, *"I expected something better, or different from him / her!" I thought he / she had higher standards than that!"* Then we hit:

STAGE 3: discouragement and / or disillusionment

And we find ourselves thinking or saying something like, *"Why should I keep trying? I mean, if he / she / they can't make it, what makes me think I can?!"* Or, we become more cynical and say, *"This whole Christian life thing is just a game, a con, a scam!"* Then:

STAGE 4: blaming and / or rejecting others

"Who needs 'em, anyway! I can make it fine on my own!" Then:

STAGE 5: getting angry

"I don't know why or how I ever got tied into that group in the first place!" To:

STAGE 6: resentful and / or bitter

"That church is nothing but a bunch of two-faced hypocrites! I live a better life than any of them!"

What often happens is that, if not resolved, in time "liquid resentment" will harden into "concrete bitterness." And both are highly toxic emotions. Better to forgive the other person than to give them that kind of control over us.

And so, then the reality of what the writer of Hebrews speaks of comes to pass: "Like a small root that grows into a great tree, bitterness springs up in our heart and overshadows even our deepest Christian relationships." [Hebrews 13:15, Modern English]

Well, what this leads us to consider is:

REALITY CHECK #2:
All Christ-followers *are capable of missteps*

Because we surely want to avoid thinking or concluding, *"Well, this or that could never happen to me!"* That's a very dangerous position to take. And why should that sort of thinking be avoided? Well, as Paul reminds us, "Be careful. If you are thinking, 'Oh, I would never behave like that' - let this be a warning to you. For you too may fall into sin." [1 Corinthians 10:12, LB] And then there's Paul's exchange with Peter in Galatians 2:10-14 where The Message renders his words: "Later, when Peter came to Antioch, I had a face-to-face confrontation with him because he was clearly out of line. Here's the situation. Earlier, before certain persons had come from James, Peter regularly ate with the non-Jews. But when that conservative group came from Jerusalem, he cautiously pulled back and put as much distance as he could manage between himself and his non-Jewish friends. That's how fearful he was of the conservative Jewish clique that's been pushing the old system of circumcision. Unfortunately, the rest of the Jews in the Antioch church joined in that hypocrisy so that even Barnabas was swept along in the charade."

And how could or should we respond? Well, perhaps the best place to begin is to...

Love 'em anyway.

Because as Jesus tells us:
"I am giving...a new commandment to you now – love each other just as much as I love you. Your strong love for each other will prove to the

world that you are my disciples." [John 13:34-35, LB]

And then:

Hear 'em out anyway.

For as another once put it, *"The first duty of love is to listen."* So, as James tells us, "Don't ever forget that it is best to listen much, speak little, and not become angry." [James 1:19, LB]
And then:

Pray for 'em anyway.

Again, as James reminds us, "pray for each other." [James 5:16, NIV] Then:

Serve 'em anyway.

That's the point Paul makes when he tells us to "serve one another in love." [Galatians 5:13, NIV]
And then:

Encourage 'em anyway.

For as Paul puts it, "Encourage one another and build each other up..." [1 Thessalonians 5:11, NIV] – as opposed to "bringing each other down", "ripping each other apart", and / or "eating each other alive"! Or, as The Message renders Paul's words in Galatians 5:15, "If you bite and ravage each other, watch out - in no time at all you will be annihilating each other..." And then:

Forgive 'em anyway.

You see, when it comes to the Christian life, "to err is human, and to forgive is company policy." Jesus tells us in the Lord's Prayer, we're to be praying "Forgive us our debts, as we also have forgiven our debtors." [Matthew 6:12, NIV]

And in any case, it's helpful to remember that forgiving them isn't for their benefit; it's for ours. To not forgive and hold something against another is like swallowing a poison pill and waiting for the other person to die.

And yet, above all else, there's...

REALITY CHECK #3:
All Christ-followers *must focus on Jesus!*

Of course, it is true that we tend to follow and focus on people, on fellow "hikers" or believers and leaders. And there's certainly a sense in which Paul encourages this where he says, "And you should *follow my example*, just as I follow Christ's." [1 Corinthians 11:1, NLT, emphasis added.] And then in yet another place he adds, "For you know that you ought to *follow our example*. We were never lazy when we were with you….It wasn't that we didn't have the right to ask you to feed us, but we wanted to *give you an example to follow*." [2 Thessalonians 3:7, 9, NLT, emphasis added.]

And then, too, the writer of Hebrews tells us to "Remember your former leaders, who spoke God's message to you. Think back on *how they lived and died and imitate* [NCV, "copy"] their faith." [NJB, "take their faith as your model"] [Hebrews 13:7, TEV, emphasis added.]

Of course, to Paul's point earlier in 1 Corinthians 11:1, if he – or any Christian or spiritual leader – stops following Christ, you stop following him or her!

That said, we do need role models; we need people to believe in and trust. However, our greatest need, our primary focus, is given by the writer of Hebrews where he says "Let us fix our eyes on *Jesus*, the author and finisher of our faith…" [Hebrews 12:2a, NIV, emphasis added.]

And why is this so critical and essential for a "fully-devoted Christ-following hiker?"

Because while others may and often do disappoint us, Jesus will never fail us, abandon us, nor let us down.

Or as the writer of Hebrews puts it, "Let your character or moral disposition be free from love of money – [including] greed, avarice, lust and craving for earthly possessions – and be satisfied with your present [circumstances and with what you have]; for He (God) Himself has said, I will not in any way fail you nor give you up nor leave you without support. [I will] not, [I will] not, [I will; a triple negative in the Greek language] not in any degree leave your helpless, nor forsake nor let [you] down, [relax My hold on you] – Assuredly not!" [Hebrews 13:5, The Amplified Bible]

THE INCREDIBLE JOURNEY
Mapping The Christian Life
-Chapter 10-
Heaven or Hell: Home at Last!

However long a journey takes – be it hours, days, weeks, months or years – and whatever distance a journey may covers – after all...

- the places we go,
- sites we see,
- people we meet,
- jobs we do, and
- goals we accomplish –

at some point the journey comes to an end and we finally arrive home.

And just as this is true for any earthly journey, it's equally if not *more* true when it comes to our spiritual journey – this Incredible Journey known as the Christian life. For as Solomon tells us, "You will turn back into the dust of the earth again, but your spirit will return to God who gave it." [Ecclesiastes 12:7, NCV]

And yet, once we die, then Solomon goes on to say that "God will judge us for everything we do, including every secret thing, whether good or bad." [Ecclesiastes, 12:14, NLT] Or, as the writer of Hebrews puts it, "We die only once [thus, there is no reincarnation, no return trips, no second chances], and then we are judged." [Hebrews 9:27, CEV] And, as Paul adds, "For we must all stand before Christ to be judged. We will each receive whatever we deserve for the good or evil we have done in our bodies." [2 Corinthians 5:10, NLT]

So in truth, the single most important question any of us will ever answer on *this* side of eternity is where we'll end up on the *other* side of eternity!

And to be sure, we do make that decision on this side of eternity. As Jesus tells us, "Unless you believe that I am who I say I am, you will die in your sins." [John 8:24b, NLT] And as John records earlier, "And all who believe in God's Son have eternal life. Those who don't obey the Son will never experience eternal life, but the wrath of God remains upon them." [John 3:36, NLT]

And since Jesus adds that: "You can enter God's Kingdom only through the narrow gate. The highway to hell is broad and its gate is wide for the many who choose the easy way. But the gateway to life is small and the road is narrow, and only a few ever find it" [Matthew 7:13-14, NLT]... Let's consider our eternal options, our "home destinations", with a sort of two-fold approach. The first involves us...

CONSIDERING OUR "WORST CASE" SCENARIO

Now, Jesus lays it out for us in a story format – and whether literal or figurative, the point remains the same. Luke records Jesus' words this way: "There was once a rich man who wore expensive clothes and every day ate the best food. But a poor beggar named Lazarus [note: this is a different Lazarus from Mary and Martha's brother by the same name] was brought to the gate of the rich man's house. He was happy just to eat the scraps that fell from the rich man's table. His body was covered with sores, and dogs kept coming up to lick them. The poor man died, and angels took him to the place of honor next to Abraham. The rich man also died and was buried. He went to hell [TEV, "Hades"; NCV, "place of the dead"] and was suffering terribly. When he looked up and saw Abraham far off and Lazarus at his side, he said to Abraham, 'Have pity on me! Send Lazarus to dip his finger in water and touch my tongue. I'm suffering terribly in this fire.' Abraham answered, 'My friend, remember that while you lived, you had everything good, and Lazarus had everything bad. Now he is happy and you are in pain. And besides, there is a deep ditch [NLT, "chasm"; NCV, "big pit"; KJV, "great gulf"] between us, and no one from either side can cross over."[Luke 16:19-26, TEV]

Then, picking up with vv. 27-31 The Message paraphrases the story like this: "The rich man said, 'Then let me ask you, Father: Send him to the house of my father where I have five brothers, so he can tell them the score and warn them so they won't end up here in this place of torment.' Abraham answered, 'They have Moses and the Prophets [i.e., Old Testament; or, in our vernacular, the Bible] to tell them the score. Let them listen to them.' 'I know, Father Abraham,' he said, 'but they're not listening. If someone came back to them from the dead, they would change their ways.' Abraham replied, 'If they won't listen to Moses and the Prophets [same as above], they're not going to be convinced by someone who rises from the dead.'"

So why is Jesus underscoring what the Scriptures [the Old Testament or Moses and the Prophets] have to say? Because as He says then, and now: "You search the Scriptures because you believe they give you eternal life. But the Scriptures [that is, Moses and the prophets – be they the major and minor ones] point to me! Yet you refuse to come to me so that I can give you this eternal life." [John 5:39-40, NLT]

So when someone says, *"I don't believe Jesus is the only way to Heaven!"* Or, *"That's just too narrow-minded...too bigoted!"* are you willing to bet your eternal life on it? I mean, if you're *right*, you have nothing to lose; however, if you're *wrong*, you have everything to lose.

Did you know that Jesus actually spends more time and space talking about Hell than He does about Heaven? In fact, 13% [or 1,850 verses] recording Jesus' words deal with eternal judgment and / or hell. I wonder why?

Oh, well, maybe He's "just trying to scare us!" Maybe...possibly...probably...hopefully.

Have you ever noticed how much air time major news networks spend warning people not travel to certain countries, or sail near Somalia, or to avoid roads during winter storms?

Are they "just trying to scare us"? Again,

maybe...possibly...probably...hopefully. It would seems that a powerful reason for believing there is a hell is the very fact that Jesus, as God, would be the One Person to be able to speak with full authority on the subject. He's actually warning us for good reason.

Now, beyond this, you've probably heard it said that, *"Well, when you die, you can't take anything with you!"* As Paul puts it, "After all, we didn't bring anything with us when we came into the world, and we certainly cannot carry anything with us when we die." [1 Timothy 6:7, NLT]

So, "nothing in, nothing out".

And yet, there is a sense in which we do take "some things" with us. I mean, as Jesus' story indicates, the rich man *does* take his memory, his relationships, and his emotions.

You see, the reason Hell is our "worst case scenario" or "least preferred option" is because rather than it being a place of wild partying with all of our drinking buddies, Jesus – and the Bible – describe it as a very real, actual and literal place of...

- pain,

- torment,
- emotional angst,
- grief,
- spiritual alienation.
- separation,
- isolation
- of being all alone,
- outer darkness, and the
- "weeping and gnashing of teeth.

It's an...
- eternal prison with no escape, no end;
- unquenchable fire; and even has
- different degrees of punishment.

And this last point makes perfect sense. I mean, we'd expect a different outcome or degree(s) of punishment for people, given the difference between, say, a Hitler or Stalin and some low-level Jesus-rejecting sinner. As Jesus puts it: "The servant will be severely punished, for though he knew his duty, he refused to do it. But people who are not aware that they are doing wrong will be punished only lightly. Much is required from those to whom much is given, and much more is required from those to whom much more is given." [Luke 12:47-48, NLT]

In other words, people who reject God's rule in

this life wouldn't want His rule in the *next*.

So, in reality, they choose Hell. As someone once said, although they may end up at the same "address", they have different "rooms". And perhaps we should also know that [initially] we were not created for Hell, nor was Hell created for us. As Jesus tells us, "Then he [God] will say to those on his left [the goats], 'Depart from me, you who are cursed, into the eternal fire prepared for the devil and his angels.'" [Matthew 25:41, NIV]

And yet, Hell is the logical choice, consequence, eternal destiny, of "home" for anyone who wants to live a life (time) separated from God. You see, God's attitude toward us [toward people] is best expressed in places like Ezekiel 33:11 [NIV] where we read, "Say to them, 'As surely as I live, declares the Sovereign Lord, I take no pleasure in the death of the wicked, but rather that they turn from their ways and live. Turn! Turn from your evil ways! Why will you die, O house of Israel?'"
And then Peter records that "The Lord is not slow in keeping his promise, as some understand slowness. He is patient with you, not wanting anyone to perish, but everyone to come to repentance." [2 Peter 3:9, NIV] And then Paul

tells us: "God our Savior...wants everyone to be saved and to come to know the truth...who gave himself to redeem the whole human race. That was the proof at the right time that God wants everyone to be saved."
[1Timothy 2:3b-4, 6, TEV]

And yet, there is a limit to God's patience. It's not like He'll restrain Himself forever. As even God Himself tells us that "My Spirit will not contend with man forever, for he is mortal." [Genesis 6:3a, NIV]

Well, since all of this represents our "worst case" scenario or least desirable eternal destiny or "home", now let's secondly begin...

ANTICIPATING OUR "BEST CASE" SCENARIO

And, as we might suspect, this means Heaven. And everyone [or almost everyone!] wants to go – and believes they *are* going – to Heaven! In fact, over my nearly fifty years of ministry, for every ten people I'd ask if they knew where they were going when they died, 9-out-of-10 would say heaven.

Of course, when I drilled down on why they thought that, their answers were all over the map! From good works, to "I've earned it", to being baptized, being religious, keeping the Golden Rule, the Ten Commandments (or at last the top 8 – whatever that means!), or being "better than most people" – especially better than those "hypocrites down at your church!" And author Randy Alcorn adds these words: *"For every American who believes he and she are going to Hell, there are 120 who believe they are going to Heaven."*

And yet, on what do people make such claims?

Well, again, they're banking on their good works, moral behavior, or religious performance and that in spite of the fact God clearly tells that "We are made right with God through faith and not by obeying the law." [Romans 3:28, NLT; TEV, "doing what the Law commands"; our good works or moral living]

This why Paul tells us that: "God saved you by his special favor when you believed. And you can't take credit for this; it is a gift from God. Salvation is not a reward for the good things we have done, so none of us can boast about it." [Ephesians 2:8-9, NLT]

And then, writing to believers, he adds that "He saved us, not because of the good things we did, but because of his mercy. He washed away our sins and gave us a new life through the Holy Spirit." [Titus 3:5, NLT]

I loved learning about this group of 9-year-olds who were asked their opinions about Heaven and how one gets there.

A boy named Jim said, *"When you die, they bury you in the ground and your soul goes to heaven; but your body can't go to heaven because it's too crowded up there already."*

Then Judy answered, *"Only the good people go to heaven. The other people go where it's hot all the time like in Florida."*

And John then added, *"Maybe I'll die someday, but I hope I don't die on my birthday because it's no fun to celebrate your birthday if you're dead."*

And Marsha said, *"When you die, you don't have to do homework in heaven, unless your teacher is there too."*

Well, dear Marsha, the good news is that there's no homework in Heaven!

And yet, there's so much that *is* in Heaven and is going *on* in Heaven and *isn't* in Heaven! For instance, we have God's Word on it that in Heaven there's no...

- temptation or sin;
- suffering or sickness;
- deformities or handicaps;
- blindness, deafness or dumbness;
- sorrow or tears;
- darkness or death; no need for
- eyeglasses, contacts, Lasik surgery
- hearing aids,
- speech therapy,
- wheelchairs or
- crutches.

Or, as Anne Graham Lotz [Billy Graham's daughter] once put it, when it comes to "My Father's House", *"There will be no betrayals or backstabbing's, slander or sex-trafficking, lies or liars....no more hospitals, death, or funerals; walkers, canes, or wheelchairs; ventilators, respirators, or IVs....no more suicide bombers or fiery infernos, broken homes or broken hearts, broken lives or broken dreams. There will be no more mental retardation or physical handicaps, muscular dystrophy or multiple sclerosis, blindness or lameness, deaf- ness or sickness. There will be no more Parkinson's disease or heart disease, food allergies or autoimmune disease, diabetes or arthritis, cataracts or paralysis, MRIs or dialysis...no more cancer or chemo or radiation; tumors or tremors or terrorizing trauma. No more guns in schools. No more guns! Or terrorists or missiles or air strikes or predatory drones or car bombs....One day you will live in the home of your dreams."*

You see, we are told that in Heaven [and / or later in the New Jerusalem] there's...

- pleasure [Psalm 16:11],
- knowledge [Colossians 2:3],
- comfort [Luke 16:25],
- love [1 John 4:8],
- joy [Luke 15:10; Matthew 25:23], and
- relationships [Luke 23]!

That at the end of our Incredible Journey we'll be met, greeted and welcomed by loved ones, saints, angels and the Lord Jesus to a "Celestial Home" described as a. . .

- garden, a
- city, a
- country, a

- kingdom with
- buildings,
- banquets,
- books, and
- [new] bodies!

Where people are laughing, playing, resting, working, and talking while...

- surrounded by physical beauty;
- enjoying incredible pleasures and happiness;
- experiencing companionship,
- reminiscing with old friends, and
- making new ones!

A place where we're with the One person we were made for in the one place we were made to be! Home at last! [Again, a great resource on this topic is the book *Heaven*, by Randy Alcorn (Wheaton: Tyndale House Publishers, Inc., 2004).

Malcom Muggeridge was right in observing that, in the end, coming to faith remains for all a *"Sense of homecoming, of picking up the threads of a lost life, of responding to a bell that had long been ringing, of taking a place at a table that had long been vacant."*

Which again is why Solomon records for us that God "set eternity in the hearts of men." [Ecclesiastes 3:11, NIV]

No wonder it seems so instinctive and intuitive to think of the afterlife, look forward to, and want to go to Heaven! It's even why we often may say it's as if we're "homesick for Eden". And so, as Jesus tells His immediate audience and us: "Don't be troubled. You trust God, now trust in me. There are many rooms. [KJV, "mansions"] in my Father's home and I am going to prepare a place for you. If this were not so, I would tell you plainly. When everything is ready, I will come and get you, so that you will always be with me where I am. And you know where I am going and how to get there.' 'No, we don't know, Lord,' Thomas said. 'We haven't any idea where you are going, so how can we know the way?' Jesus told him, 'I am the way, the truth, and the life. No one can come to the Father except through me.'" [John14:1-6, NLT]

So, belief in Heaven – or what you believe about Heaven and Hell – is really based on what you think or believe about Jesus.

Now again, to many this sounds rather "narrow

minded", as if believing this makes one bigoted and / or intolerant. Well [again!] it's God's Heaven, so it seems only right that He gets to set the "entrance requirements". Besides, when you think about it, all religions make "exclusive truth" claims; they can all be wrong; they can't all be right.

So – again – what it all comes down to is what we believe, and what we do, about Jesus. And in the "free marketplace" of ideas about truth, it all comes down to which leader or founder makes the best claims and can back 'em up. And, as Jesus adds, "No one who has faith in God's Son will be condemned. But everyone who doesn't have faith in him has already been condemned for not having faith in God's only Son." [John 3:18, CEV]

Or, as The Message puts it so plainly, "Anyone who trusts in him is acquitted; anyone who refuses to trust him has long since been under the death sentence without knowing it. And why? Because of that person's failure to believe in the one-of-a-kind Son of God when introduced to him."

So allow me to end with a question: When *your* "journey" ends where will *you* spend eternity?

This isn't a trick question.

Honestly: which "scenario" [best case or worst case / most preferred choice or least preferred choice] represents your eternal home? Because in the end, though becoming a real Christian is childlike, it isn't childish. Choosing Heaven as your eternal home *is* as simple as "A-B-C"! That is, one must:

Admit

Admit what?

That you are a sinner and need Jesus Christ to forgive you of your sins.
By the way, the Bible never says we're as bad as we can be. All of us know people who are worse – or better– than we are.

And yet, what the Bible does claim is that we are as bad *off* as we can be – that is, we're dead in our sins. As Paul tells us, *"As for you, you were dead in your transgressions and sins."* [Ephesians 2:1, NIV, emphasis added.] And then he adds, "For all have sinned; all fall short of God's glorious standard ....For the wages of sin is death, but the free gift of God is eternal life through Christ Jesus our Lord."   [Romans 3:23; 6:26, NLT] Then:

Believe

Believe what?

That Jesus died on a cross in your place, for your sins, as the substitute taking the punishment for what you deserve: death for your sins. As Paul puts it, "But God showed his great love for us by sending Christ to die for us while we were still sinners." [Romans 5:8, NLT] And then:

Call

Call what? Or who?

It's you, and me, and anyone who calls upon His name – Jesus – to save us; to save you; forgive you; to come into your heart and take up residency in your life. Again, as Paul tells us, "For 'Anyone who *calls on the name of the Lord* will be saved.'" [Romans 10:13, NLT, emphasis added.] And the Apostle John adds, "But to all who *believed him* and *accepted him,* he gave the right to become children of God. [John 1:12, NLT, emphasis added.]

So, why not do that today? What's holding you back?

Remember – Paul puts it rather pointedly when he writes that "Now is the time of God's favor, *now* is the day of salvation." [2 Corinthians 6:2b, NIV, emphasis added.]

So why not let this moment in time be the "first day" of the rest of your life when your Incredible Journey with Jesus Christ really begins? It can be. Just let this prayer be yours:

"Dear Jesus, thank You for making me and loving me, even when I've ignored You and gone my own way. I realize I need You in my life and I'm sorry for my sins. I ask You to forgive me. Thank You for dying on the cross for me. Please come into my heart and life and make me a new person inside. Help me to understand what it means to truly belong to You. As much as I know how, I want to follow You for the rest of my life. I accept Your gift of salvation. Please help me to grow now as Your child."

And, if you prayed these words and meant them, and you now know Jesus Christ is your personal Lord and Savior, let someone know that you know Jesus Christ for yourself!

I'm sure they'll be rejoicing with you!

After all, as Jesus tells us, "There is joy in the presence of God's angels when even one sinner repents." [Luke 15:10, NLT] Or, as The Message renders His words, "Count on it – that's the kind of party God's angels throw every time one lost soul turns to God."

What an incredible way to end our Incredible Journey!

Or better – for you – to begin your own incredible journey!

REFERENCES & FOOTNOTES & PAGE

2- **World Equestrian Games©**- international championships held every four years for equestrianism, administered by the Federation Equestre Internationale (FEI)©

- **Girl Scouts of America© 100th Anniversary,** -founded by Juliette Gordon Low, March 12, 1912in Savannah, GA

- **St. Louis 200th anniversary Lewis and Clark Exposition©**- commissioned by President Thomas Jefferson in 1803, objective to explore and map newly acquired territory and find a route across the western half of the continent, establishing an American presence, before other world powers tried to claim it.

3- *Knowing God* is a book by the British-born Canadian <u>Christian theologian</u> <u>J. I. Packer</u>, and is his best-known work, having sold over 1,000,000 copies in North America alone.[1] Originally written as a series of articles for the *Evangelical Magazine*, it was first published as a book in 1973 by Inter-Varsity Press, and has been reprinted several times.

20- **George Clooney- American Actor, director, screen writer, producer.**

-**"Up in the Air"©- 2009-** Directed by Jason Reitman, Executive Producer- Michael Beugg, Distributed by Paramount Pictures©™,

25- **Dr. Jekyll and Mr. Hyde©**- written by Robert Louis Stevenson 1886, London, England, Longmans, Green & Co™©.

29- **Frank Sinatra-,** American singer, actor, director, and producer

- **a. The Voice** – (The Voice of Frank Sinatra©) Sinatra's first album, released on Colombia Records©™,

-b. My Way©- lyrics- Paul Anka, Reprise Label™©

- *The Parent Trap* is a 1961 Walt Disney film. [It stars Hayley Mills, Maureen O'Hara and Brian Keith in a story about teenage twins on a quest to reunite their divorced parents. The screenplay by the film's director David Swift was based upon the 1949 book *Lottie and Lisa* (*Das Doppelte Lottchen*) by Erich Kästner

30- John Greenleaf Whittier-American poet (1807-1892)

-A quoted excerpt from Whittier's'- poem- "Maud Muller"©

31- Dr. Karl Menninger, psychiatrist- an American psychiatrist member of the Menninger Family, © founding family of Menninger Clinic™®/Foundation©® in Topeka, KS, an author of many books.

- Charles R. Swindoll; sermon 6-2015; "Who Indeed Knows?" www.insight.org

 - NASA –National Aeronautics and Space Administration®©- formed July 29, 1957, A U.S. government facility for space exploration and the like.

58- C.S. Lewis-(1898-1962) British novelist, poet, theologian and lecturer.

-2nd quotation – Overcoming the Dark Side of Leadership, page 177;Authors Gary L. McIntosh and Samuel D. Rima; Baker Books 11/2007

40- Google Maps©- World Mapping Services© provided by Google Inc™®©. - Mountain View, CA

Yahoo© Maps- World Mapping Services© provided by Yahoo©®™, Inc. Sunnyvale, CA

Map Quest©- a World Mapping Service© provided by AOL©™®, a division of Verizon©™®

Rand McNally©®™- RM Acquisition©™, LLC, d/b/a Rand McNally©™

 AAA™®©-American Automobile Association™©, is a branded member of AAA Life Insurance Co. ©™

41- Lao Tzu – (6th-5th B.C.) Chinese philosopher, founder of Taoism

- Yogi Berra- (1925-) retired American baseball catcher, manager & coach.

42- Peter Jennings- (1938-2005), Canadian-American journalist and news-anchor.

- The American Agenda©™®- American Broadcast Co (ABC) ®™©a division of the ABC Entertainment Group©™®/The Walt Disney Corp. ®™©- nightly news series hosted by the late news-anchorman-Peter Jennings

- Barna Research Group©- (see notation on #86)

45- KJV 1611- (British) Cambridge University Press©, Cambridge, England, the 1611 King James Bible is part of the Public Domain usage

48- American Bible Society©-(ABS) –Bible publishers, NYC

49- Life Application© NIV or NLT- Tyndale House Publishers© Carol Stream, IL & Zondervan Publishing© Grand Rapids, MI /Harper Collins Publishers© Nashville, TN

50- Josh McDowell- Evidence That Demands a Verdict© (first published 1972- Campus Crusade Pubs©., Nelson Word Pubs©-1986)–

- Norman L. Geisler and Ronald M. Brooks- When Skeptics Ask© [Baker Pubs©., 2013] {Norman L. Geisler, Ronald M. Brooks} are American evangelists, authors and theologians

- Lee Strobel- (former atheist), an award-winning editor of The

Chicago Tribune©, a NY best-selling author of more than 20 books and a professor at the Houston Baptist University®.

57- Ravi Zacharias, quoted by Lee Strobel in his book The Case For Faith. Ravi Zacharias is an Indian born, Canadian-American Christian apologist, author of many Christian books.

58- C.S. Lewis quotation from Mere Christianity, Originally published 1943

63- C.S. Lewis quotation see note #58

-Possibly a paraphrase of A.W. Tozer quote from "The Pursuit of God"

61. Wayland Baptist University©- a coeducational Baptist University, located in Plainview, TX,

62- Kilwins Chocolate Factory©- located in Petoskey, Mi, creating fine chocolates, candies and ice cream since 1947, www.kilwins.com ™

74- Chris Tomlin {American born contemporary Christian musician, worship leader, songwriter and author} - Raise the White Flag? - Passion-White Flag?

77- Vertical Limit©-American film, directed by Martin Campbell, Colombia Pictures©, December 08, 2000

-Mission Impossible 2©- An American film, (based on original Mission Impossible television series by Bruce Geller, 1966-73, DesiLu Prod©. Paramount Television©, CBS Television Ditr.©) directed by John Woo, Paramount Pictures©, May 26, 2000

- Dame Julie Andrews-(1935-) An English film and stage actress, singer, author, theatre director and dancer.

- The Sound of Music©-An American musical based on the memoirs of the Story of the Trapp Family Singers, directed by Robert Wise, March 02, 1965- USA, March 29, 1965-UK, 20th Century Fox©

83- George Barna-(1955-) pollster and founder of The Barna Group©,

- Barna Research Group© is an evangelical Christian polling firm based in California.

- The Power of Team Leadership©, page unknown by George Barna, Waterbook Press. ©™, a div. of Randomhouse, Inc.™

88- Prince Charles (1948-)-Charles Philip Arthur George- Prince of Wales, Duke of Rothesay or Duke of Cornwall

- Princess Diana (1961-1997), Diana Francis Spencer (Lady Diana Spencer) later became- Princess of Wales, {also known as Duchess of Cornwall, Duchess of Rothesay and Countess of Chester}.

 90- Samuel Taylor Coleridge- (1772-1834), English poet, literary critic and philosopher - Friendship is a Sheltering Tree

103- Warren W. Weirsbe, Real Worship, page 20. Published by Baker Books 1986

117- School children's blizzard- January 12, 1888- Americas worst recorded weather assaults, killing 235 people.

121- St. John of the Cross (1542-1591)- Religious founder, priest (Carmelite Order) and Doctor of the church, and poet

122- See footnote 3

124- See footnote 3

129- **Aldous Leonard Huxley** (26 July 1894 – 22 November 1963) was an English writer, philosopher and a prominent member of the Huxley family. Huxley was mysticism, in particular, Universalism. By the end of his life, Huxley was widely acknowledged as a humanist, pacifist, and satirist. He later became interested in spiritual subjects such as parapsychology and philosophical one of the pre-eminent intellectuals of his time. He was nominated for the <u>Nobel Prize in Literature</u> in seven different years. Quote source unknown.

130- Scott Peck- The Road Less Traveled published 1978 by Simon and Schuster.

133- Animalplanet.com©- US television cable channel, launched October 01, 1996, owned by Discovery Communications®,

136- Author unknown. Most likely a paraphrase from "River of God"; authors Douglas D. Priest and Stephen Burris; Wipp and Stock Publishing 4/2002.

- Pulitzer prize – founder American-Hungarian born-Joseph Pulitzer created award for outstanding achievements in newspaper, online-journalism, and musical compositions. Prizes are awarded every year in 20 different categories.

- By Ellen Goodman, copyright 1991, Boston Globe Newspaper Company article titled: Battling Our Culture Is Parents Task.

- Lamaze- The Lamaze Technique popularized by the French Obstetrician Dr. Fernand Lamaze.

- Parent Teachers Association© (PTA©) or PTSA-Parent-Teacher-Student Association©, is composed of parents, teachers, students and /or staff to help facilitate parental participation in school activities. A non-profit formerly based in Chicago, IL and now based in Alexandria, VA. Founded February 17, 1897 in Washington, D.C. by National Congress of Mothers©- Alice McLellan Birney and Phoebe Apperson Hearst.

137- MTV™-launched August 01, 1981 owned by Viacom Media Networks©,-NYC consisting mainly of music videos, comedy shows, movies and other music related programming.

194

140- Gallup Poll©-founded in 1935 by George Gallup, headquartered in Washington, D.C., is an American researched based performance-management consulting company.

141- Ouija boards™- An occult-based game first commercially used in 1890, Trademarked in 1891 by the Kennard Novelty Co.

- Star Wars© the Movie, Sith Lord Darth Maul©-Launched in 1977 by George Lucas, LucasFilm™ and ILM™, Sith Lord-Darth Maul- a character in the Star Wars Episode 1: The Phantom Menace™©-directed by George Lucas, LucasFilm™, 20th Century Fox©

144- Cartoon character Pogo© quotation- author Walt Kelly, launched October 04, 1948, Syndication- Post-Hall Syndicate™©, Simon & Simon Publ. ™©, Fantagraphics Books™©, Spring Hollow Books™©,

158- Jim Bakker (1940-)-James Orsen"Jim" Bakker, an American Televangelist, former Assemblies of God© minister and former television host of the PTL™ (Praise The Lord Club™- Trinity Broadcasting Network™)-Club™©

- Reverend Moon-(born Mun Yong-myeong-1920-2012), was a Korean religious leader who founded the Unification Church, considered to be a cult leader in some religious circles.

- Jim Jones-(1931-1978) was an American born religious leader and founder of the People Temple. He's best known for the mass-suicide in November 1978 of its 909 members in Jonestown, Guyana.

- Applewhite's "Heaven's Gate"- Marshall Herff Applewhite, Jr (1931-1997) was an American Cult leader who founded what is commonly known as "Heaven's Gate". He created and led 39 people in a mass suicide in San Diego, CA.

- Halley's Comet-Discovered by Edmond Halley (1656-1742) in 1680...-

- David Koresh (1959-1993) The American leader of the Branch

Davidians religious sect,

160- The Torah- is the main core of the Judaic teachings and traditions. It includes the rabbinic commentaries, the first five books of twenty-four books of the Tanakh.

164- Pastor Chuck Swindoll quotation through page 158

179- Hitler- Austrian born, Adolf Hitler (1889-1945), the authoritarian Chancellor of Germany from 1933-1945

- Stalin- Russian Empire (1878-1953), primarily known as the General Secretary of the Communist Committee of the Communist Party of the Soviet Union

182- From an article in the Los Angeles Times by K. Connie Kang, published October 25, 2003. First paragraph.

- Booklet titled How Can We Know That We'll go to Heaven? by Randy Alcorn, paragraph one, published 1/1/2007 by Good News Publishers and Crossway Books.

184- **Anne Graham Lotz** (born **Anne McCue Graham** May 21, 1948) is an American Christian evangelist. She is the second daughter of evangelist Billy Graham and his wife Ruth Graham. She founded AnGeL Ministries, and is the author of 11 books, of which her best known is *Just Give Me Jesus*

180- See footnote 182

- C.S. Lewis books

The Last Battle© quotation-(Harper Collins Publ. ™©)"The New Narnia"© quotation and "the Unicorn"© quotation- page numbers for quotations of the Last Battle.

181- See footnote 9

ABOUT THE AUTHOR

DAVE MARTIN is the proud father of two children and seven grandchildren. His journey includes working in the marketplace, from sales to factory life; in ministry he served as a youth evangelist, student pastor, associate pastor, teaching pastor, lead pastor and transitional pastor in small-to-large churches in Missouri, Hawaii, and Kentucky. He's also served as an adjunct faculty member of three colleges, and became the president of one. He holds a Master of Divinity from Southwestern Baptist Theological Seminary, and a Doctor of Ministry degree from Covenant Seminary. Currently he is writing, serving churches in the greater St. Louis area, mentoring younger pastors, and planting a new church in St. Charles, Missouri. He and Terry, his bride of forty seven years, reside in Wentzville, Missouri.

You can reach Dr. Martin at: souldr@charter.net

Author Dave Martin